THE PURSUIT OF HAPPINESS

The Pursuit of Happiness

Blessing and Fulfillment in Christian Faith

Sarah Heaner Lancaster

WIPF & STOCK · Eugene, Oregon

THE PURSUIT OF HAPPINESS
Blessing and Fulfillment in Christian Faith

Wipf & Stock
An Imprint of Wipf and Stock Publishers
199 W. 8th Ave., Suite 3
Eugene, OR 97401

www.wipfandstock.com

ISBN 13: 978-1-60899-902-6

Manufactured in the U.S.A.

I could not do any of the work that I do without the constant support of my husband, Kermit.

I dedicate this book to him, in gratitude for the happiness we have shared.

Contents

Acknowledgments

T HE MATERIAL FOR THIS book is all original, but I have presented some of these ideas in previous settings. I wrote a short article "Happiness: A Word for Our Time," in *Journal of Theology* 109. I have also made presentations on John Wesley's understanding of happiness in a workshop for those who teach United Methodist Doctrine held at Duke Divinity School of Duke University and in the Systematic Theology Group of the Oxford Institute of Methodist Theological Studies (2007). The positive response I received from these presentations encouraged me to develop the ideas further.

A few people deserve thanks for reading my manuscript and offering feedback. Lisa Withrow, Robin Knowles Wallace, and Gregory S. Clapper all made suggestions that were very helpful. I also had the opportunity to read Greg Clapper's manuscript for *The Renewal of the Heart Is the Mission of the Church* while I was writing this book. The ideas in that book prompted ideas for my own. In addition, I had some interaction with Ellen Charry during this time. Her work on *God and the Art of Happiness* sharpened some of my thinking. I am grateful as well for the time I spent in the Summer Wesley Seminar at Duke Divinity School in 2005. At that time while researching another project, I found some resources from the seventeenth and eighteenth centuries that proved also to be useful for this project.

1

Introduction

P EOPLE WANT TO BE happy. Nothing could be more obvious, and yet this common and evident goal is not as easy to achieve as it is to desire. We know we want to be happy. We may even think that we ought to be happy—believing that something is wrong if we do not feel good. Almost everyone, though, has some time in her or his life when happiness is difficult. For some, that period may be relatively short, but for others it may endure for years. Realizing that there is a disconnection between what we want to feel and what we do feel can make us even more unhappy. Conversely, when life is going well and we feel satisfied with it, we may take happiness for granted, perhaps even believing we have a right to have it (and not just the right to pursue it). In either case, whether we suffer from a lack of happiness or assume that it is ours by right, people believe happiness to be of importance. It is a central goal of human life.

The search for happiness is both ancient and modern. It is ancient because it was a topic for Western philosophy millennia ago, and it is modern because the way we conceive of and expect happiness in the twenty-first century is quite different from generations of the distant past. This book will explore happiness as an ancient pursuit with contemporary meaning, and it will do so by trying to understand this common human desire within the framework of Christian faith.

It may seem odd to attempt a book on happiness from a Christian perspective. For a few decades at least (although only a short time in the whole scope of Christianity), Christians in the United States have preferred the word *joy* to the word *happiness* when talking about their positive experience in Christian faith. It is common to hear Christians relegate happiness to "the world" and speak of it as a far lesser goal, calling people to a deep joy instead.[1] The insight that there is something different about what Christian faith offers than what most people think of when they pursue their happiness is a good one, but giving up the word *happiness* in order to talk about that difference seems to me to be a mistake. First, both *happiness* and *joy* have a history of use in English translations of the Bible, so there is no scriptural reason to put them in competition with each other. Second, if *happiness* is the word that most people actually use in their daily lives, then it is the better point of engagement for talking about what Christian faith has to offer, especially for people who are not already in the church. Third, abandoning the word *happiness* can blind us to resources in the Christian heritage for talking about the deep experience that Christians want to share. Christians of previous centuries used both the words *happiness* and *joy* to talk about their experience with God, and they were aware that the word *happiness* put them in line with a long philosophical tradition from which they could draw to explain what they meant. They did, of course, feel free to develop the idea of happiness in a way suited to Christian faith, but they did not shy away from saying that happiness and Christian faith go together. In the light of this rich history, it makes no more sense to give up the word *happiness* than it does to give up the words *redeem* and *redemption* because we also use those words to talk about coupons. It may be useful, though, to identify the kind of happiness we mean by calling it "Christian happiness," and I will do so at times in this book.

This book, then, does not attempt a general theory of happiness. It is concerned, rather, to show the specific way that Christians have talked about happiness in God. Neither is it an attempt to survey all Christian reflection on happiness.[2] The breadth that I seek is about how to cover the many facets of Christian happiness itself. I find it useful to focus pri-

---

1. This assumption forms the basis for a recent popular Christian book by Wagner, *Myth of Happiness*.

2. For a study of greater breadth in the Christian tradition, see Charry, *God and the Art of Happiness*.

marily on a particular figure to see how he addresses multiple concerns within a developed perspective. So after providing some introduction to the topic in Christian faith more generally, I will focus on the work of John Wesley as an example of a theologian who took happiness as a topic for serious theological reflection. I am not making any claim about his own personal happiness, rather I am looking at the theological concept of happiness that he held. Although John Wesley's work is of interest to me because I stand in a tradition that regards him as founder and mentor, I think his work can be instructive beyond the specific Wesleyan/ Methodist tradition. When John Wesley and his brother Charles began organizing and equipping Methodists in the eighteenth century, it was not their intention to start a new church, much less a "branch" of Christianity. They called the gathering of Methodists a "society," to indicate that the members were not separating from the church but were coming together to deepen their commitment to discipleship.[3] In that spirit, I take John Wesley's reflections on happiness to belong, not simply to a particular tradition, but to the whole church. It is precisely because Wesley's understanding of happiness is less well known than that of, say, Thomas Aquinas that he may promote new avenues of reflection on the topic. I offer this account of his thinking as an example of how the riches of Christian faith may contribute to happiness, and I hope that this example will encourage others to explore Christian happiness using the resources in their own traditions. Of course, I would also like Christians who see themselves as Wesleyans or Methodists to regain and use this heritage in John Wesley's work.

Because his reflection was undertaken in the context of a lively movement that involved many ordinary, faithful Christians, Wesley did not produce a merely abstract theory, but rather arrived at his conclusions with the help of testing in the lives of real people. In this sense, his reflection on happiness is a genuinely practical theology. It is my hope that reflection on the topic in our present time would also have such relevance to Christians who may be uninterested in theory but who seek a deep and fulfilling relationship with God. Reclaiming the Christian practice of reflection on happiness could potentially enliven churches and make sharing faith a delight.

---

3. See Davies, "Introduction," 1–29.

It has long been recognized that the centerpiece of John Wesley's theological reflection was salvation. If one holds a superficial understanding of happiness, the topic may seem frivolous next to salvation, and to some it may even seem damaging insofar as it distracts from the serious matter of being saved. Wesley, though, did not have a superficial understanding of happiness that could be considered either frivolous or distracting. He offers a deep and meaningful description of happiness that shows it to be, along with holiness, the essence of salvation itself. The hunger to be made whole and the hunger to be happy are related, and this book finds in John Wesley's theology an attempt to help us feed these deep hungers with that which will make us truly whole and therefore truly happy. In the way of salvation that Wesley preached, our happiness as human beings is connected to fitting ourselves to the kind of life that God intended for us in our creation. We gain happiness by aligning our spirits with God, because only then do our lives fulfill the purpose for which we were made.

Wesley does not, though, offer his description of happiness all at once in a systematic argument. In fact, he has not always been regarded as a theologian of consequence (even by Methodists) because he did not produce a grand theological system. Instead, he wrote short sermons and other kinds of materials that were intended to convey theological ideas to ordinary people in a way that would matter for their daily lives. He often wrote situationally, addressing matters as they arose (for instance to answer charges made by his critics or questions that emerged among Methodists), rather than systematically—moving formally from one sermon to another to build a case. Forming an understanding of his theology requires using many resources. The main resources that I use to uncover his theological understanding of happiness are his sermons. At times, I also draw from his journals or other works. I even turn to his brother Charles Wesley's hymns occasionally to provide examples of what Methodists would have learned about happiness through their singing.

Clearly, happiness matters to people, but the kind of happiness that we seek also matters. In a "happiness culture" that encourages people to pay attention to and seek for those things that make them feel good, the loss of those things or the failure to attain them can lead to frustration and even depression. If those things we think will make us happy do not, then what are we to do? The history of reflection that informs Wesley's own work thinks of happiness as deep human fulfillment, so it is less about pleasure and absence of pain than it is about living an integrated life that has meaning. That understanding of happiness has much to commend it in a society that promotes seeking and satisfying personal desires. The Wesleyan tradition also has significant practices to draw from that aid the pursuit of this kind of happiness. Thinking about Christian happiness, properly understood, as the goal of life with God both sets the direction for spiritual formation and provides the driving force behind participating in those practices that will lead to that formation.

As interested as he was in the personal fulfillment that individuals long for, Wesley recognized that none of us lives in isolation. Our lives are so intimately connected with others that our own fulfillment, our happiness, includes happiness of others. There is, then, a social dimension to his theology that is essential. Authentic lives take shape in relationship, not only as we demonstrate our Christian love through actions toward others, but also as we develop personal Christ-like qualities through the way we interact with those around us. Wesley's work is not simply individualistic, even though it offers powerful spiritual guidance to individuals, and it can serve as a helpful resource and counsel for a time when our connectedness with one another is becoming more and more apparent.

Reclaiming a theology of happiness can help Christians find language for expressing the fulfillment they receive through their faith that is especially pertinent to our time. The search for happiness has taken a new form in psychology, and insights from that discipline are being widely dispersed through popular culture. The field of psychology is contributing to an understanding of fulfillment, and some of the findings resonate with practices of Christian faith. A theology of happiness, though, will have to go beyond psychology. It presses beyond transient feelings of personal satisfaction to the ground of life, which alone can satisfy completely.

Using the language of happiness can inform many aspects of the church's work. At a time when many no longer know the classic language of salvation (for instance, the words *justification* and *sanctification*) happiness can offer a vocabulary for sharing the good news that could enliven evangelism and inform preaching. To use the language of happiness, though, requires care and thoughtfulness to avoid falling into superficial understandings that can do more harm than good. A theology of happiness acknowledges sorrow, as well as trials in life, but puts them in a context in which they can be borne with grace. Taking happiness as a serious topic of reflection can result in a practical theology, one which provides a pattern for living that connects us with God and allows us to live the life of integrity for which we long. Christians can learn to satisfy our deepest hungers in God and share a way of finding the fulfillment humans so desire.

John Wesley's theology provides an entry point for an understanding of Christian faith that can be developed further in light of the questions of our time. He is important for this topic not because his thoughts should be taken as definitive, but rather because he has touched on so many issues that matter. His reflection also took place in a movement that offered a place to test and revise certain ideas. Though it may be unfinished, the reflection he started provides a starting point that has both depth and breadth. He has been called a practical theologian because he sought to make theology accessible and meaningful to ordinary Christians. His reflection on happiness can provide an orientation for a theology that continues to be practical for a new generation of Christians. This book intends to enable the possibility of thinking with him about a topic of common interest that has potential for illuminating Christian spiritual life in the twenty-first century.

Before talking about Wesley, though, I set the stage for his reflection in two ways. First, in chapter 2, I take a brief look at reflection on happiness in the early centuries of philosophy and Christian theology. Drawing from Greek and Roman philosophy, theology developed an idea of what happiness is that partially reflected its roots but that was also modified to fit the emerging theology of the early church. Augustine's major influence in the development of Christian theology in the West extends also to the understanding of happiness. Happiness also featured prominently in the work of Thomas Aquinas. The language used by these theologians to talk about being happy in God carried with it the idea of blessing, and they clearly rooted the concept in relationship with God. Second, in chapter 3, I examine some of the reflections on happiness that introduced ideas into English thinking that would have influenced Wesley. During the seventeenth and eighteenth centuries, happiness became closely associated with pleasure in the wider culture, and its pursuit became a major preoccupation. Meanwhile in theology, happiness was linked closely with holiness, seeking an internal experience that would confirm genuine relationship with God.

The exploration of John Wesley's understanding of happiness takes shape in three movements. First, in chapter 4, I show how important the concept of happiness was for Wesley's theology. Happiness was God's intent for us in our creation, but it was lost in the Fall. Salvation restores our happiness, so the idea is at the heart of soteriology. The pursuit of happiness, then, is not simply a pursuit of pleasure. Rather, it is the pursuit of the restored image of God. Second, chapter 5 shows the substantial link in Wesley's thinking between happiness and holiness. For Wesley, the way to happiness is found through holiness, and he organized the Methodist movement in accordance to what he understood to be the biblical method for the art of happiness, namely, cultivating a life of holiness. For Methodists, then, the pursuit of happiness was followed by growing in inward and outward holiness. Finally, chapter 6 shows that Wesley thought of happiness as more than feeling good. In fact, he developed the notion of "heaviness" to explain how Christians may yet be happy in God even when they face situations that bring great sadness. Christian happiness is not defined by lightness of mood, and the loss of such a mood does not necessarily result in the loss of Christian happiness. A holy life that fittingly displays God's love brings a satisfaction that can last through difficult times.

With Wesley's concept of happiness in mind, chapter 7 presents an overview of some of the notions of happiness that are competing for attention of the public. The field of psychology has begun to study positive emotions, including happiness, and its findings are having an impact on common understanding of what happiness is. The psychological understanding of happiness, though, does not match precisely with the theological understanding that I want to reclaim. Critical engagement with emerging ideas about happiness will be important for showing the importance of a theological concept for speaking adequately about the meaning of human life.

Finally, in chapter 8, I offer some brief reflections on what ministry practices fit with a theology of happiness. I describe some characteristics of a congregation where Christian happiness is flourishing. Although I do not have the expertise to make specific recommendations about practices, I mention practices that I believe would reflect and promote the blessing and fulfillment that belong to Christian happiness.

2

Blessing and Fulfillment

I**T SEEMS SIMPLE AND** natural to want to be happy—a desire so obvious that stating it seems unnecessary. If the desire is obvious, though, the way to gain happiness is not. As important as it is to us, a happy life is not guaranteed. Perhaps because it can be elusive, happiness has, not only been the common longing of ordinary people, but also a central topic of reflection for many great thinkers in Western society. As a simple but uncertain aim, the topic poses a problem for life that many have sought to explain. Before looking at how the quest for happiness developed in Christianity, it is helpful to recall some of the history that shaped reflection in the Western world, and therefore Christian theology itself.

ANCIENT PHILOSOPHY

Philosophy means "love of wisdom," and much of the wisdom that was sought in ancient Greece was about how to live a good life, not only rewarding to the one who lived it, but also praiseworthy because others could see its value. A central component of a good life was "happiness,"[1] although identifying just what constituted happiness was part of the

---

1. In this chapter, I will often put the words *happy* and *happiness* in quotation marks to serve as a reminder that the English usage may not be a straightforward rendering of the meaning in Greek.

intellectual quest that philosophy undertook. Just as English can use several words to speak of "happiness" (for instance, joy, cheerfulness, gladness, enjoyment), Greek also had several words that have been translated into English as "happy," especially *olbios*, *makar*, and *eudaimon*. The question of how to translate these Greek words into English is itself an important issue. "Happy" may not always be the best rendering because the English carries with it a connotation of subjective feeling that the Greek does not always intend to convey. It is important, then, to have some sense of what these Greek words communicated in their time. The vocabulary available to the ancients gives insight about the conceptual framework in which philosophical reflection took place. The questions that they had about "happiness" were largely shaped by the options for understanding it that were available to them.

In the religious context of ancient Greece, each of the three words above was tied in some way to the gods. In Homer's epics, *makar* is used to describe something about the gods, who are immortal, untroubled by storms or famine, and therefore able to live lives of ease.[2] To be *makar* meant that the gods had a kind of unshakeable security and serenity. This is a state for which humans in a changeable and changing existence can only long, but a human could be called *makar* to the extent that his or her life resembled the security and serenity represented by the divine ideal. By the fifth century BCE, Greek literature showed this difference by utilizing the word *makarios* ("one who shares to a certain extent in the distinction of being *makar*")[3] to describe humans and generally reserved *makar* for the gods.[4] To share with the gods in this way was to be "blessed"—the English word sometimes used to translate the Greek. In other words, a *makarios* human life was a reflection of the blessed lives of the gods.

Olbios also found its meaning in connection with the gods. In its earliest use, it meant being without grief or gloom caused by misfortune, and in the religious context of the time, one avoided misfortune by not angering the gods. It became easy to extend this negative meaning (not being in disfavor) to a positive meaning (being in favor), and a clear sign of being favored by the gods was wealth and social position.[5]

2. DeHeer, *Makar—Eudaimon—Olbios—Eutyches*, 4–6.

3. Ibid., 31.

4. Ibid., 83–87. DeHeer points out in these pages how imprecise translation into English and other modern languages is partly because the context and concepts are so different from our own.

5. Ibid., 32–38.

Olbios, then, began to be connected to material wealth and status as a sign of divine favor.

The third word mentioned above, *eudaimon*, shows a clear etymological connection between happiness and divine favor. This Greek word combines the prefix that means "good" or "well" (*eu-*) with the word for "spirit" or "divinity" (*daimon*).[6] In other words, life runs smoothly for a person when some god or spirit is well disposed toward that person.

This cluster of words in Greek indicates some of the areas of concern for philosophers who considered human "happiness." First, there is a clear distinction between the security of divine life and the vulnerability of human life. Second, the words indicate that human prosperity, security, and therefore peace of mind depend on circumstances that are often not under a human's control, but rather lie within the purview of the gods. Third, a "happy" life, then, can be very vulnerable to outside forces. This vulnerability that makes "happiness" uncertain and impermanent prompted a great deal of reflection among philosophers.[7] Closely related to "happiness" is the notion of "luck," expressed in Greek as *tuchē*, or good luck, *eutuchē*. Luck was not, though, simply chance. It refers to outside forces, not of one's own agency but possibly of the agency of the gods, that affect one's life. The connection between luck and happiness is that those things that happen beyond one's own direct control have a great deal to do with the satisfaction, enjoyment, and value that a person can have in life.

At one time, the English word "happy" reflected more of this insight than it does now in common usage. "Happy" and "happiness" are related to the word "happen" through their common root: the Middle English word "hap," which meant "luck" or "chance." The connection between these two words is that when good things happen (by luck or chance) then one is happy. Some event that takes place, not necessarily of one's own making, is beneficial and pleasurable, so one feels contentment, euphoria, or some other positive emotion. Daily use of these words,

---

6. Over time, the *daimon* of *eudaimonia* has often come to be seen as part of the self (in other words, the "spirit" is one's own spirit). This drift in connotation is in keeping with the emphasis on self-sufficiency that developed in philosophy, but it is most likely that the more ancient origin of the word had in mind the gods. For an explanation of the more recent usage, see Sarot, "Introduction," 9.

7. Nussbaum examines "the aspiration to rational self-sufficiency in Greek ethical thought: the aspiration to make the goodness of a good human life safe from luck through the controlling power of reason" (*Fragility of Goodness*, 3).

though, has generally reduced "happy" and "happiness" to the positive feeling and does not always call to mind the connection of that feeling to what "happens." In the ancient world, though, the connection was felt keenly, and it posed a major line of questioning for thinkers who contemplated human existence.

One of the options in Greek thinking for what it meant to have a good life was that one had good luck most of the time instead of bad luck, in other words, the events over which one had no control were mostly beneficial to one's condition. In this view, a person could tell by the things that had happened to her or him whether she or he had been favored by outside forces or not. Since favor could turn to disfavor and vice versa, the end of life could be quite different from the years that preceded it, so one could even say a life could not be declared "happy" or "favored" until it was over. Herodotus makes this point when he tells of a meeting between Solon, an Athenian statesman, and Croesus, the king of Lydia. Croesus asks Solon, who has traveled much, to report on who is the "happiest" (the Greek uses a form of *olbios*) person he has seen. Expecting that he himself will be named because of his wealth, Croesus is surprised that Solon gives this honor to a man who has died in battle, followed closely by two brothers who died after performing a great service for their mother. The noble ends of these lives secured a judgment of "happy" or "favored" for them, whereas Croesus was only presently enjoying benefits that could be lost at any moment. Indeed, after this conversation, Croesus loses the "happiness" that he enjoyed through a series of misfortunes.[8] The tale Herodotus tells displays the vulnerability of human fortune and suggests "happiness" or "favor" is something that can only be pronounced of a human life at its end, when death secures its permanent status and one's whole life can be evaluated. No one can be truly "happy" in this sense while still alive. The "happiness" that constituted a good life, in this way of thinking was more of an objective judgment than a subjective feeling.

But what would it mean if a person had more bad luck than good? Did that mean that the life had not been worth living? And even if the sum total of events were positive, some individual events, such as the death of a loved one, could be devastating. Would a significant loss

---

8. Herodotus *The History* 1.30–34. The Greek uses a form of *olbios* most of the time, but does introduce *eudaimon* in chapter 32, the word that will be picked up later by many philosophers.

outweigh a larger number of smaller benefits? Indeed, precisely because life was vulnerable, because good things were fragile, and because no one was immune to reversal of fortune that could threaten all one held dear, this vulnerability to negative events pressed home the question of whether a life could be considered "good" or "excellent" or "happy" apart from outside forces. Rather than embrace Solon's judgment that no one alive can yet be called "happy," many philosophers began to define the "happiness" of the good life in a very different way. Rather than being subject to the favor of the gods, or dependent on fortune or luck, many began to think of the "happiness' of the good life as something that belonged within the realm of human capacity. The standard word used in this reflection was *eudaimonia*, a form of the third Greek word— *eudaimon*—discussed above.[9]

With this shift, the "daimon" or "spirit" that was deemed to be good was no longer an external deity but one's own spirit, or character. Not suffering internal disturbances due to changes in one's circumstances was the key to *eudaimonia*, and key to avoiding internal disturbances was having the right understanding of one's nature and the world.[10] Even with this shift away from outside forces and toward one's own internal experience, the meaning of *eudaimonia* is not quite what most English speakers usually mean by "happiness." Many scholars have suggested that the word *eudaimonia* is better translated into English as "human flourishing" or "well-being" rather than "happiness" because in our time "happiness" has the connotation of an emotional or psychological state.[11] When Greek philosophers debated what constituted an excellent life, they had something else in mind than simply how a person feels.

9. Philosophers could use not only *eudaimonia* but also at times forms of the word *makarios*. The question of whether any single philosopher used these words interchangeably or intended a clear distinction between them is complicated. The general tendency, though, in philosophy was to seek the good life in *eudaimonia* as self-sufficiency. Nussbaum argues that Aristotle allowed more vulnerability in the good life than did Plato. See chapters 11–12 in *Fragility of Goodness*. In doing so, Aristotle often argues against opponents who would claim internal character is sufficient by itself for the good life, so self-sufficiency was clearly an idea that had great influence at the time.

10. Trapp even calls *eudaimonia* and its Latin equivalents in Roman philosophy "rational happiness" because the functioning of the intellect is so central to it. See *Philosophy in the Roman Empire*, 31. As we shall see in subsequent chapters, reason is an element of other emotions, as well.

11. On the difficulties in translating the Greek *eudaimonia* into English, see Nussbaum, *Fragility of Goodness*, 6 note.

Some evaluation of the life was still important, even if that evaluation did not have to wait until death.

The surviving record of Greek thought shows that philosophers were deeply preoccupied by questions such as these, and they came to different conclusions in their reflections. Although many sought *eudaimonia*, an excellent life—a life that was both praiseworthy (external evaluation) and rewarding (internal state) for one who had learned to value the right things—exactly what constituted an excellent life was debated. Ancient philosophy spanned several centuries and the debate included many different voices. Major schools of thought had their roots in ancient Greece but continued over centuries into the Roman Empire.[12] A few examples will show how far ranging the search for an excellent life could be.

Epicureans turned to pleasure as the standard for goodness, and therefore happiness. This approach has often been misunderstood to reduce happiness to immediately satisfying sensual desires (a better word to describe this approach to pleasure is "hedonism"). Epicureans recognized different kinds of pleasures, though, some leading to greater happiness than others. The point in this approach is simply to acknowledge that pleasure is preferred to pain, and that a person attains an excellent life by seeking and finding the most lasting pleasures. A different kind of approach, taken by the Stoics, was to seek control over one's state of mind. The key to a "happy" life was having the wisdom to see that those things which most people value have instead indifferent worth. If riches or health, for instance, are not as important as people think they are, then one could remain tranquil through either gain or loss. Skeptics did not explicitly seek *eudaimonia*, but they did consider what would make for the most fulfilling human life. They sought freedom from internal disturbance, not by cultivating a single way of thinking, but by suspending judgment on all ways of thinking, particularly about what might be "good" or "bad."[13] Many philosophical streams worked in the direction of placing the excellent life more under one's own control with less dependence on outside forces.

The dominant philosophical tradition that later shaped Christian thinking, though, comes from Plato (often through neo-Platonism) and

12. Trapp, *Philosophy in the Roman Empire*, 1–2.

13. For a fuller account of ancient philosophy and its search for *eudaimonia*, see Parry, "Ancient Ethical Theory." For the Latin versions of these ideas, see Trapp, *Philosophy in the Roman Empire*, 28–62.

Aristotle. Each of these thinkers undertook formal reflection on how to secure "happiness" (*eudaimonia*) without simply depending on external events. From these philosophers, not only Christianity, but Western culture has learned much about what constitutes an excellent life. While they each have their own distinct ideas, they also share some common concerns. For instance, "happiness" is not simply feeling good. Instead, it is living in accordance with our nature as humans; in other words, the deepest fulfillment comes from fulfilling what it means to be human, in contrast to falling short of who we are supposed to be (for instance, by simply following lower desires instead of controlling them).[14] Reason plays a key role in human nature because it distinguishes us from the animals and it connects us to the divine.

In order to live in accord with our nature, one must understand what human nature is, and then one must learn to value properly the things that will truly fulfill it. Aristotle, in particular, considers how *eudaimonia* depends on cultivating enduring character traits (virtues) that humans ought to have. That task is not always easy, and it may involve struggle with desires or circumstances that work against the traits we want to cultivate. For instance, one may want to have an honest character but find oneself in a position where lying would bring great benefit, and the situation is made more difficult if one's desire for that benefit is great. That struggle to be honest in those circumstances will surely not "feel good," but it counts toward having an excellent (happy) life when, by prevailing in the struggle, it leads to a deeper development of honest character.

The ancients knew that the things we think will make us happy do not always do so. The legacy that they left in Western thinking has set the course for enduring questions. The search for happiness consists in large part in learning to identify what will bring true happiness. Human beings have desires, passions, or appetites that we seek to gratify, but we also have rationality that helps us govern those powerful aspects of our nature so that they do not simply control us. We are happy when we direct our lives toward what is truly good rather than direct (or misdirect) them toward lesser goods. The wisdom that the philosopher seeks

14. For instance, in the *Phaedrus*, Plato describes the soul as two winged horses controlled by a charioteer (reason) and says, "If now the better elements of the mind, which lead to a well ordered life and to philosophy, prevail, they live a life of happiness and harmony here on earth." The word Plato uses that is translated as "happiness" in this case is actually *makarion*. Later in the same speech, he uses *eudaimon*. Plato, *Euthyphro, Apology, Crito, Phaedo, Phaedrus*, 501.

is to know what is truly good so that she can prioritize and arrange her activities, purposes, thoughts, and so forth, in order to gain it. An excellent or happy life is a life ordered toward that which will truly fulfill it. So philosophers must ask, What is the highest, most permanent, most fulfilling goal that one can seek so that one's life will be truly satisfied when one finds it? One can only be happy when one knows how to answer that question.

CHRISTIAN THEOLOGY

Christian theologians answered that question with the God of Jesus Christ. God alone was truly good, God alone was the highest value, so God alone could truly satisfy. A happy life was one that was ordered toward God. The goal of human life that philosophy had set—well-being that comes from fulfilling one's nature—could, with some adjustments, also express the goal of Christian life. The necessary adjustments, though, are important for understanding the distinct understanding of "happiness" that Christian theologians developed.

As Christianity spread into the Gentile world, some theologians who had been educated in Greek philosophy used their education in the service of Christian faith. Clement of Alexandria, for instance, argued in book 1 of the *Stromata* that it was appropriate to adopt written composition (as the philosophers had) to preserve and disseminate theology. Although the truth in Scripture was superior, philosophy had its place in preparing minds for that truth. Many ideas in Greek philosophy, then, corresponded to Scripture, which could then supplement or correct the philosophy as needed. One such idea was "happiness" as *eudaimonia*. Clement offers a discussion of the ways that many philosophers see the end (goal) of human life, and as he describes them, some had less resonance with Christian truth (Epicurus, the Stoics) and some more (Plato and Aristotle).

According to Clement, Plato had understood that the end of happiness was to be like God as much as possible, and Aristotle connected this end to virtue. To Clement's mind, philosophers such as Plato and Aristotle had caught glimpses of the truth. They were, though, simply expressing what Scripture said in fuller form. We are, indeed, to be like God, and Scripture shows that we become so by imitating Christ, who is himself the Wisdom of God. The heart of this imitation is indeed virtue (known by Christians as righteousness and holiness). What Scripture tells us that philosophers cannot is that such virtue is attained by obeying the commands of God.[15] The philosophers were right that to be happy we must fulfill our natures as human beings, and that fulfillment can only take place when we order our lives toward the highest good, but, for Clement, the highest good is the God that Christians worship, and the properly ordered life is a life of obedience to God's commands.

Theological engagement with philosophy was not always so direct. Still, even when it did not refer to philosophy, theology in the first centuries tended to adopt the basic orientation toward the end of human life that Clement expressed. Because they were willing to let Scripture correct philosophy, theologians preferred language related to the Greek word *makarios* rather than *eudaimonia* to talk about the good or excellent life. To see why, recall that in ancient Greek *makarios* carried with it the idea of blessing, or being blessed as the gods were blessed. "Blessing" can refer to honoring the gods as holy, or it can indicate the gods' conferring a gift as they share something of their holy selves with humans. To be "blessed" then was connected to being holy. This language had become scriptural because the Septuagint had often used *makarios* to translate the Hebrew ʾ*ashar* or ʾ*ashrei* (for instance in Ps 1:1). This language was also used in the new writings that were being circulated among Christian churches (for instance in Matt 5:1–11).

The word's connection with the divine—no longer "the gods" but "the God" of scriptural revelation—fit precisely what Christians understood life to be about. Instead of seeking fulfillment in self-sufficient *eudaimonia*, Christians looked outside themselves for fulfillment in God. Indeed, the notion of "salvation" implies that one needs help from the outside for one's security. Whereas many philosophers had viewed outside forces as threats (and the pagan gods could be capricious), Christians understood there was one outside force which alone was dependable and fulfilling, and that was the God of Jesus Christ. Language related to *makarios*, then, did not display vulnerability but rather the most secure satisfaction of the good or excellent life that one could have.

Because the only "outside force" that made a Christian *makarios* was God, other forces did not have the power to undo this blessing—which is the gift of grace that enables us to share in the life of God. Clement of Alexandria writes, "Salvation does not depend on outward things, whether they are many or few, small or great, splendid or lowly,

15. Clement of Alexandria *Stromata* 2.22.

glorious or mean, but upon the soul's virtue, upon faith, hope, love, brotherliness, knowledge, gentleness, humility and truth."[16] Clement could affirm that being rich in virtues and poor in passions would enable a person to bear the loss of material possessions graciously.[17] A person who can do so is "blessed [*makarizomenos*] by the Lord."[18] Blessing, then, is not calculated according to material signs of favor, as it had been when the Greeks first reflected on happiness. Rather, it is seen in the attitude—reflecting divine serenity gained by knowing and valuing what is truly good—with which one bears the loss of material goods. Similarly, Clement of Rome wrote,

> How fortunate [*makarioi*] are those who obey these commandments! Even if they suffer evil for a brief time in this world, they will reap the imperishable fruit of the resurrection. And so the one who is pious should not be despondent over miseries suffered at present. A more fortunate [*makarios*] time awaits him![19]

In light of what we have learned about the word, a better translation might be "A more blessed [or happy] time awaits him!" It is this understanding that allowed Christians to extend the word *makarios* to martyrs, who suffered greatly and lost their very lives, but who endured their agonies by remaining focused on the truly good.[20] The blessed or "happy" life, then, is not an untroubled life. It is rather one that is righteous and holy because it has known and clung to God, the highest good of all. Only this life could bring the deepest fulfillment, even in the face of enormous loss.

In Western Christianity, Latin replaced Greek as the language of theology, but as it did so, the connection between blessing and fulfillment remained. The Latin Vulgate Bible had translated forms of the Greek *makarios* into forms of the Latin word *beatus*. Notably, Jesus's words in Matthew 5:1–11 and Luke 6:20–22 are known in English as the beatitudes because in Latin the sayings begin with the Latin word *beati*. The Latin, like the Greek, means both "blessed" and "happy." The language *beatus* had also been used by Roman philosophers to describe human

16. Clement of Alexandria *The Rich Man's Salvation* 18.

17. The phrase is *hileō tē gnōmē*, which Butterworth translates as "with a cheerful mind."

18. Clement of Alexandria *The Rich Man's Salvation* 16.

19. Clement of Rome *Second Letter of Clement to the Corinthians* 19.3–4.

20. See, for instance, Marcion *Martyrdom of Polycarp* 2.

life lived toward its highest goal, the *eudaimonia* of Greek philosophy.[21] As language that was both scriptural and philosophical, it quite easily made its way into theological reflection.

Augustine of Hippo (354–430 CE), who deeply influenced the development of theology in the West, was trained in philosophy and sought to articulate Christian faith in a way that would convey its truth and importance with high intellectual rigor. Like Clement of Alexandria, Augustine believed that the chief good was the God of Jesus Christ, and that human nature could only be fulfilled by relationship with this God. Also like Clement, Augustine followed the model of philosophy in his theological reflection. His early work *De Beata Vita* ("On the Happy Life") embraces the philosophical theme of "happiness" as the goal of human life. It also presents this theme in the style of classical philosophy. He uses the dialogue form to present his reflection, and the dialogue touches on common philosophical questions, such as the nature of true happiness and the means of its attainment.[22]

Augustine continues to talk about happiness in later works, but in them, he moves beyond standard philosophical argument to connect happiness more closely to the Christian narrative. In book 14 of the *City of God*, Augustine discusses human nature by describing how human beings were created to be and how the Fall has kept us from living as God intended us to live. Humans were created with free will, so they could freely obey God and freely remain in right relationship with God. Adam and Eve, however, used their freedom to disobey God.[23] As a result, they and their descendants lost the freedom to govern their desires and actions that would have enabled them to order their lives toward God. Human nature, which was meant to be free and obedient, became damaged so that it was in bondage and disobedient.[24] Though human nature could only be satisfied by relationship with God, it was unable after the Fall to live in right relationship with God and so was constantly dissatisfied. Human beings cannot be happy without being righteous,

---

21. Seneca wrote *De Vita Beata* as his account of how being in harmony with one's own nature leads to the happy life, and Cicero also used *beatus* in his writings.

22. Brown has compared Augustine's *De Beata Vita* with Seneca's *De Vita Beata* and Cicero's *Tusculan Disputations* in *S. Aureli Augustini De Beata Vita*.

23. Augustine *City of God* 14.11–13.

24. Ibid., 14.15.

and they cannot be righteous without the help of God.[25] That help comes through Jesus Christ, the only true mediator who can help humans attain a life of bliss (*vitam beatam*).[26]

Augustine, then, connects the fulfillment of human nature to the work of Jesus Christ for our salvation. None of us can live the life we wish because our desires and actions are not entirely under our control. We want and strive to attain things that cannot give us true happiness.[27] Only through Jesus Christ can our nature be restored to what God intended it to be, so happiness is indeed a blessing, coming to us from outside ourselves and fulfilling us as nothing else can. In *On the Trinity*, Augustine says that blessedness (*beatitudo*) belongs to the very nature of God, so there is a connection between what we receive from God and who God is.[28] We are blessed when we enjoy the very blessedness of God. As he says in the *Confessions*, "The happy [*beata*] life is this—to rejoice to thee, in thee, and for thee. This it is and there is no other."[29] In Augustine's hands, "happiness" moves from a philosophical goal to be understood through argument and sought through right thinking to become a central idea in the Christian narrative.

For Augustine, if there had been no disobedience, life in the Garden of Eden would have been marked by joy (*gaudium*) in God and felicity (*felicitas*), because all needs were met and there was no disharmony. Through the Fall, though, this original happiness was lost and human nature is unable by itself to regain it. God's action is required to restore the right functioning of human nature so that true happiness is again a possibility. In Augustine's thinking, the fulfillment of human nature is still the key to happiness, but now that fulfillment depends on salvation through Jesus Christ. Happiness that has been lost and is then restored comes to us as a blessing (conferring a gift) to be received with gratitude and humility. Though Augustine does not make the connection explicit, the idea of grace certainly comes to mind. For Augustine, true human happiness is not possible through our own efforts and so is not under our control; rather, it comes to us as grace and blessing when our lives are deeply connected to God's own life. In making this move, Augustine

25. Ibid., 14.25.

26. Ibid., 9.17.

27. This point will be discussed more thoroughly in chapter 4.

28. Augustine *On the Trinity* 8–15.

29. Augustine *Confessions* 10.22.32 (trans. Outler).

has both retained and transformed the ancient prephilosophical idea that happiness depends on something outside ourselves. In Augustine's hands, though, this reliance on something outside us does not make us insecure. Instead the one outside force on which human happiness depends is the utterly reliable God of Jesus Christ: happiness is secure in the security of God.

Centuries later, informed by Aristotle, Thomas Aquinas developed an extensive theological system that named happiness as the "end" or "goal" of human life. In dialogue with the philosopher, as well as with Christian theologians, Thomas Aquinas works carefully through many questions regarding what happiness is and what is required to attain it.[30] Is wealth happiness? No, wealth is only a means to happiness, not happiness itself. Is honor happiness? No, people honor another person for his or her excellent character, but since an excellent life is a happy life, honor comes because of excellence or happiness. Is fame or glory happiness? No, fame and glory depend on what other people know or think about you, but one's own happiness cannot depend on what other people know or think. Thomas proceeds to eliminate power, bodily good, and pleasure as candidates for what happiness is. Not even the good of the soul is happiness itself. True happiness benefits the soul and comes to us through the soul, but it is something outside the soul. Happiness cannot be identified with any created thing. For Thomas, true happiness is *beatitudo*, again calling to mind blessing or blessedness, and it is found in God alone.

So if happiness is *beatitudo*, how can a person attain it? Thomas does not provide a "how to" manual, but he states that we gain true happiness by seeing or contemplating God. When we direct our wills to attain the proper end, rather than something lesser, we will attain happiness. That is, if we make something like wealth or power the goal for living, then we will direct our thoughts and actions toward getting it. But those things will disappoint us. Alternatively, if we make contemplation of God the goal for living, then we will direct our thoughts and actions toward God, who will not disappoint us. The more we arrange our lives so that we keep this goal in mind and work toward it, the happier we will be. As long as we are in this present life, though, even happiness in God is not complete. For one thing, we can forget our experience of God or be distracted by tasks that do not allow time for contemplation. For

30. Thomas Aquinas, *Summa Theologiae*, 2.1, q. 1–5.

another, even our best moments of contemplation in this life are partial compared to the kind of direct participation in God's life that will be available to us after death. This direct experience of God's life is sometimes called the "beatific vision." For Thomas, true happiness is only finally and fully gained when we live eternally in God. Because of this, the attainment of true happiness is not possible under our own natural power, but only through the salvific mediation of Jesus Christ.

Christian theologians both learned from Greek philosophy and modified it so that they could talk about happiness in ways that corresponded to their knowledge and experience of Christian faith. While Greek philosophers worried about the vulnerability of happiness because of outside forces and often sought its security in self-sufficiency, Christian theologians believed the only truly secure happiness came from outside oneself, but it was truly secure because it was grounded in God. With this security, one could bear all sorts of losses (even to the point of death) without compromising one's deepest fulfillment. This fulfillment was more rewarding than the enjoyment of any lesser good could be. The steadfastness of the martyrs who held to God alone could be recognized by other Christians as praiseworthy or "blessed" (sharing in the blessedness of God) and could serve as a witness to others of that which is truly good.

The Christian view became that God makes us happy because we were made for God. To be fit for this relationship that satisfies our deepest longing, humans need to follow God's commands. Philosophical "virtue" became Christian righteousness and holiness. Out of all of God's creation, human nature is uniquely created for this relationship. Our lives find their meaning and purpose when they are lived for God, and so happiness does not simply come from "outside" us—it fulfills us deeply "inside." These basic convictions come through over and over again in the history of Christian theology. The search for happiness in Christian faith is a search for God.

3

Happiness and Misery

ALTHOUGH THE ANCIENT IDEAS explored in the previous chapter have persisted and exert their influence still today, the intellectual upheavals that began in the seventeenth century also left their mark on how people thought about happiness. The Protestant Reformation that began in the previous century had challenged the structures and authority of the Roman Catholic Church, subsequent religious wars brought extreme hardship, and "security" in any form—whether of knowledge, authority, or happiness—was hard to come by. As old ideas collapsed, new ones took their place. For instance, as institutional authority in the church was challenged, emphasis on the ability of the Holy Spirit to speak directly to individuals emerged as its alternative. Not only in the church, but also in many fields of learning, people began to question received wisdom from the past (not simply accept it as authority because of its antiquity) and to look to experience for guidance. Reason also gained prominence, culminating in the eighteenth-century Enlightenment.

Both philosophy and theology were affected by developments such as these, and while the search for happiness continued, it gained different nuances during this time. Although certain fundamental theological commitments remained, they were expressed in language that came from and spoke to the times. Throughout Europe, the struggle to come to terms with the new questions posed by new developments led to significant contributions by many thinkers, but those who wrote in English have particular importance for understanding John Wesley's views of happiness that will be explored in subsequent chapters. This chapter will examine some of the ideas that were already present in England and that shaped Wesley's own thinking.

JOHN LOCKE

One of the crucial figures in seventeenth-century English philosophy was John Locke. He lived in a time when science was adopting specific procedures of empirical observation as its method for learning about the world, and Locke explored how sense experience might become the foundation, not simply for science, but for knowledge in general. Locke opposes what he takes to be the common view that certain ideas or principles are innate (that is, that they are simply in the mind naturally), and instead argues that ideas are gained through the senses. We learn the idea of sweetness by tasting sweet things, hardness by feeling hard things, yellow by seeing things that are yellow, and so on. Some ideas are gained through more than one sense (for instance, we learn the idea of motion both by seeing things move and by feeling ourselves move), but the point remains that these simple ideas are gained through experience rather than already residing in the mind.

Added to sense experience is the mind's capacity to reflect on those experiences. Furthermore, the mind also has the capacity to reflect on how it reflects on these sensations. From thinking about its own processes, the mind gains ideas about things such as thought, volition, and memory. The mind is then capable of combining simple ideas into complex ideas.[1] Locke's work was focused on developing a theory of knowledge (epistemology) that suited the new empiricism of the time, but it also had a shaping effect on the understanding of happiness.

Simple ideas are distinct from one another. Sweetness is distinct from bitterness, hard is distinct from soft, yellow is distinct from white. One of the most basic distinctions that we sense is the difference between pleasure and pain. On the pleasure side of these sensations, we have satisfaction, delight, happiness, and so on, while on the other side we have uneasiness, anguish, misery, and so on. The desire to gain pleasure and

---

1. Locke, *An Essay Concerning Human Understanding*, 2.1–7.

to avoid pain provides motive for our actions, even (and perhaps especially) for seeking God. Locke even suggests that the degrees of pleasure and pain in worldly life are there because of God's own purpose. We desire happiness, and any lack of happiness, whether through pain or incomplete pleasure, makes us uneasy because the desire is not met. God alone can provide the joy that will completely eliminate uneasiness, so the uneasiness we feel in this life serves to lead us beyond imperfect things to God.[2] Even if they start with sense experience, both happiness and misery can be understood as more than bodily pleasure and pain because mental life also has its pleasures and pains. Grounding happiness in sense experience, though, sets all our pleasures on a continuum, so happiness in God is the continuation and culmination of ordinary experiences, not a qualitatively different goal.[3]

Our uneasiness does not always lead us to God, even though it should, because we can settle for immediate pleasures rather than seeking lasting ones. Our judgment about what will make us happy is not always accurate, but we should have the freedom to pursue that which we believe will make us happy.[4] This understanding of happiness and freedom could be seen to justify pleasure-seeking in any form, but Locke calls attention away from passing pleasures to lasting ones. Anyone who considers not simply temporary happiness, but "infinite happiness" will understand that it is gained by living a good life, rewarded by God in the next life, even if this life brings pain.[5]

Although Locke's argument about happiness as pleasure sounds more Epicurean than Platonic or Aristotelian because it argues from

2. Ibid., 2.7, paragraphs 1–6, and 2.21, paragraph 40.

3. McMahon shows how Locke was influenced by Epicurean ideas through Pierre Gassendi. He also speculates that Locke's emphasis on pleasure and pain in this life came from contact with radical Protestants, who talked about earthly happiness. McMahon understands Locke to have legitimated the pursuit of happiness in this life by connecting it both with science and with God's own plan for creation. See McMahon, *Happiness: A History*, 175–88.

4. Locke, *Essay Concerning Human Understanding*, 2.21, see especially paragraphs 48, 55, 57, and 73. In paragraphs 44 and 52, Locke uses the phrase "pursuit of happiness," the famous phrase that Thomas Jefferson used in the Declaration of Independence of the United States from England as a substitute for "property" in Locke's own phrase "life, liberty, and property." Garry Wills notes that this substitution was neither introducing a new idea nor implicitly criticizing Locke but rather expresses a rather common idea of the time. See Wills, *Inventing America*, 240–47.

5. Locke, *Essay Concerning Human Understanding*, 2.21, paragraph 72.

pleasure rather than from what constitutes human nature, he has none-
theless tied happiness to virtue. In fact, he goes so far as to say at one
point that "the pursuit of true and solid happiness" does fulfill our "intellectual nature."[6] He has retained, then, some of the substance of the
philosophical and theological tradition before him even though he has
built the case on quite different grounds.

The linking of happiness to pleasure and desire became the common assumption of many writers of the time. When Samuel Johnson
defines happiness in his famous dictionary, the first definition he gives
is "felicity; state in which the desires are satisfied."[7] John Gay, an English
moral philosopher, defined happiness as "the sum total of pleasure."[8]
To speak of happiness in terms of pleasure and satisfying desire placed
the measure of happiness in a person's own experience. It also became
common to accept Locke's idea that happiness and misery presented two
fundamental alternatives in human life.

PURSUIT OF HAPPINESS

Misery had been the harsh reality of the lives of many people. If happiness was satisfied desire, many desires went unsatisfied. Disease, want,
disability, and death were constantly present. For years, Europe had suffered greatly with plagues and wars. Conditions for life, though, began
to improve in the eighteenth century.[9] With the Industrial Revolution,
products became plentiful and inexpensive enough that—even though
hardship did not disappear—more people could satisfy more desires
than previous generations had been able to do. By the eighteenth century, then, the British population had both a philosophy that sanctioned
pursuing happiness and increasing means to do so.[10] In fact, happiness
became a topic of great interest—explored in Alexander Pope's *Essay on*

6. Ibid., 2.21, paragraph 52.

7. Johnson, *A Dictionary of the English Language.*

8. Gay, "Concerning the Fundamental Principle of Virtue or Morality," section 4.

9. McMahon, *Happiness: A History,* 205–6. McMahon states that the population of
Europe began rising in the second half of the eighteenth century because of longer life
spans due to improved food production.

10. Flanders, *Consuming Passions,* 42–44. Flanders argues that the increase of goods
that marked the nineteenth century actually began in the eighteenth. The number of
shops increased before industrialization, indicating to her that the desire for goods
drove the Industrial Revolution rather than the presence of more goods in the Industrial
Revolution driving the desire.

Man and made a moral principle by Francis Hutcheson. Neither interest in happiness nor increased goods, though, could ensure happiness, and Samuel Johnson explored the tension between satisfied desires and lingering uneasiness in his novel *History of Rasselas: Prince of Abyssinia.*

Johnson wrote *Rasselas* as he learned that his mother was in danger of dying. Johnson had never had an easy life, and he had often struggled with poverty. The publication of *Rasselas* provided Johnson with money for his mother's funeral.[11] In this time of distress, Johnson wrote of a prince who lived in a valley that "supplied its inhabitants with the necessaries of life," and once a year the emperor paid a visit to give his children "delights and superfluities" so that "every desire was immediately granted."[12] This place of gratified desires was known as "the happy valley."[13] One prince in the valley, though, found himself "miserable" because "pleasure has ceased to please."[14] When told that he would value his happiness more if he saw the miseries of the world, the prince resolves to escape the valley and see what has so far been hidden from him. Eventually, he plots and executes an escape, taking with him his sister Nekayah and Imlac, a man of learning who was well traveled before coming to the happy valley. Imlac tells the prince that the Europeans have many "comforts of life," but even they are not happy because "[h]uman life is everywhere a state in which much is to be endured, and little to be enjoyed."[15]

The prince is looking for a choice of life that will make him happy, but in their travels, the prince and princess encounter over and over again ways of life that would seem to give happiness but do not. The novel ends without a tidy resolution, but the princess at least learns that the choice of life is less important than the choice of eternity.[16] She decides to devote her life to learning and teaching so that she can "raise up for the next age models of prudence, and patterns of piety."[17] In her case at least, the uneasiness of this life has pushed her to contemplate the choice between infinite happiness and infinite misery in the next life

11. Birkbeck, "Introduction," 9–33.
12. Johnson, *History of Rasselas*, 38–39.
13. Ibid., 40.
14. Ibid., 43.
15. Ibid., 66–67.
16. Ibid., 157.
17. Ibid., 158.

that Locke had described and to live—and to encourage others to live—a good life that will secure the former.

EXPERIENCE AND HAPPINESS IN CHRISTIANITY

Of course, the choice of eternity had always been a concern in Christian theology, and it was common to think (as Locke had done) of this alternative in eternity as being between happiness and misery. If happiness in this life did not completely satisfy, and if true and solid happiness could be gained only after this life when one was finally with God, then the key to happiness was salvation. The conditions for salvation, then, were of paramount concern and were the subject of considerable debate after the Reformation. In the religiously contentious England of the seventeenth century, arguments were waged in print over holiness and faith as requirements for salvation.[18]

Although the theologians who were concerned about salvation were not "empiricists" in the scientific sense of this word, experience became an important test for knowing one's standing before God. Not sense experience, but some inner experience provided knowledge about one's salvation. With this emphasis on experience, theology echoed to some extent the epistemology of the time. Just two years before the restoration of the monarchy with Charles II, William Allen (a General Baptist) wrote *A Glass of Justification* in which he argued that a person was justified by an "active lively working faith,"[19] that is, one that led to doing works in "sincere obedience."[20] God would reward those who diligently sought and sincerely loved God.[21] To know whether one's faith was the kind that justified, one needed to try or test it at the "court of conscience."[22] Holding a glass (or mirror) up to oneself to see the truth about one's diligence and sincerity was an important exercise in Christian living.

18. A notable example of this kind of argument: Edward Fowler wrote *Design of Christianity*, in which he argued for the need of inward, real righteousness. John Bunyan replied in a pamphlet (*A Defence of the Doctrine of Justification by Faith in Jesus Christ*) to say that Christians are justified only by Christ's imputed righteousness, not by any real righteousness on their part. Richard Baxter articulated a position close to Fowler's in *How Far Holinesse Is the Design of Christianity*. This debate contains much of the terminology that would later shape Wesley's theology.

19. Allen, *A Glass of Justification*, 26.

20. Ibid., 21.

21. Ibid., 81.

22. Ibid., 165.

As a good Protestant, Allen is sure to say that works follow from and never substitute for faith. But he also argues that works done in sincere obedience really matter. God designed this means of salvation for us because God was concerned not only with our happiness (eternally being with God) but also with our holiness. By requiring us to be holy (righteous or virtuous), God is demonstrating God's own divine holiness. Allen, like Clement, understands that Christian happiness is connected to imitating Christ, and we imitate him by following God's commands. It is not just the activity of obeying, though, that matters. The sincerity with which one obeys is a crucial quality for true holiness. We share most fully in the holiness of God when we truly want to be godly. For Allen, happiness and holiness are linked together because God desires both for us.[23] The saints have always shown saving faith by depending on God for their happiness as well as for the power to walk in God's ways (holiness).[24] In this way, happiness is still a gift and blessing and not merely the result of our action. Allen's themes of living a holy life that makes us fit to be in God's holy presence—where alone we gain true happiness—and of testing justifying faith (lively so as to lead to holiness) in one's conscience became themes that were echoed in many later writings.

While Allen wrote in a period when Nonconformists were in a relatively good position in religiously contentious England, Puritan theologian John Flavel published *The Touchstone of Sincerity* in a time when Nonconformity was greatly repressed. He encourages every Christian to self-examination in order "to give all diligence to make his calling and election sure."[25] Prosperity, observes Flavel, increases the number who may deceive themselves and others with their profession of faith; adversity, though, "purges the church" of these unregenerate persons.[26] Trials have a different effect on the godly and the ungodly.[27] Neither the godly nor the ungodly seek adversity, but when the ungodly face adverse conditions, their hearts are shown to be false. The godly, in contrast, are

23. Ibid., 68–69.

24. Ibid., 109.

25. Flavel, *Touchstone of Sincerity*, A4. This same entreaty is made by Nathaneal Culverwel in *The White Stone*, 97. Flavel picks up many of the themes of Culverwel's treatise.

26. Flavel, *Touchstone of Sincerity*, 18.

27. Flavel's discussion of the difference between the godly and the ungodly constitutes much of the book. See especially 86–103.

proved to have sincere hearts because they turn to God in adversity and seek what God wants to correct in them through it. The difference between the two may not be apparent on the outside, but the nature of one's own heart will be apparent to any person who searches deeply inside. Flavel says, "This knowing in ourselves is by inward sensible experience, taste and feeling, which is abundantly satisfying to the soul."[28] Trials, then, bring assurance of salvation, assurance such that "it is impossible to keep him from his transports of joy, as it is for a man to forbear laughing when he is tickled."[29] Assurance of salvation, then, would bring happiness even now because of the knowledge of happiness to be gained in a future life with God. Flavel says, "as the work [of self-examination] is full of difficulty, so your discovery of your sincerity will be full of sweetness, and joy unspeakable," and "'tis your eternal happiness that stands or falls with your sincerity."[30]

By the eighteenth century, testing one's standing before God in one's own sincerity had become a matter of considerable interest, and some debate. Religious publications alluded often to assurance, conscience, and sincerity.[31] Some thought that sincerity was more important for a Christian's salvation than orthodox belief, and this principle could even be extended to speculation about whether "virtuous heathen" might be saved from damnation by their sincerity in some way.[32] In this religious climate, gauging one's internal spiritual state clearly had great importance.

JONATHAN EDWARDS AND RELIGIOUS AFFECTIONS

The emphasis on interior testing to gain assurance set a tone for Christian thinking that crossed the sea to the New World. In one sense, testing by experience was in keeping with the rational goals of the Enlightenment. In another sense, though, the experience used for the test was described in terms of "affections" rather than "reason."[33] The place of "affections"

28. Ibid., 172.

29. Ibid., 41.

30. Ibid., 221 and 222.

31. See for instance, Bragge, *Of Undissembled and Persevering Religion*, and Doddridge, *The Rise and Progress of Religion in the Soul*.

32. See discussion in Balguy, *Silvius' Examination of Certain Doctrines*.

33. The eighteenth-century shift in language to "emotion" reflected a growing tendency to divide reason from emotion and oppose the two. Edwards ascribed a certain

in the Age of Enlightenment was an uneasy one. The century that champtioned reason began to lose the rich vocabulary that had been in place to talk about emotional life. Features of life described by words such as passion, affection, sensibility, temper, and so on eventually were gathered up under the single word "emotion."[34] Much intellectual nuance was lost in this transition, but those features of life did not disappear as the vocabulary to describe them did. In fact, the Age of Enlightenment was also an age of revival, with powerful emotional expressions of religious experience occurring both in England and in the colonies. In the New World, Jonathan Edwards reflected on the emotional expressions of faith, known then as "religious affections" in order to present a way of discerning those that were based on the genuine gracious activity of God from those emotional effects that were not.

Edwards states in his preface the questions to be undertaken in *A Treatise Concerning Religious Affections*:

> what are the distinguishing qualifications of those that are in favor with God, and entitled to his eternal rewards? Or, which come to the same thing, What is the nature of true religion? And wherein do lie the distinguishing notes of that virtue and holiness, that is acceptable in the sight of God?[35]

The need for such discernment is great because true religion and false religion are often mixed, a situation that Edwards believed allowed Satan to divide Christians and thus squelch revivals. Very early in the *Treatise*, Edwards establishes, "True religion, in great part, consists in holy affections." This claim is rooted in 1 Peter 1:8, which Edwards explains were words written to early Christians facing persecution. Their response to the trying times proved them to have true religion, and the essential operations of this true religion were love and joy.[36] Happiness, then, is placed right at the heart of genuine, saving Christianity.

Because Edwards uses the word "joy" so often, some language use needs to be made clear. It has become common in Christianity today to relegate the words *happy* or *happiness* to secular or mundane feeling and to

---

rationality to affections, so he does not display this tendency. His use of the word *affections*, though, does show his orientation to religious life to be different from those who increasingly stressed reason in religion.

34. Dixon, *From Passions to Emotions*, 98–134.

35. Edwards, *A Treatise Concerning Religious Affections*, 84.

36. Ibid., 93–95.

reserve the word *joy* for that which is truly Christian. English usage in the eighteenth century (and previous centuries) made no such distinction.[37] They had, as we shall see, the same concern to distinguish true happiness from false happiness (one could as easily say—as Edwards did—true joy from false joy), but they did not make this distinction by using the word *happiness* to signal something lesser. For Edwards, *joy* and *happiness* are synonymous, and they both genuinely express true religion.

Edwards links the affections to the will or inclination. We are inclined toward those things that are pleasing and inclined away from those things that are displeasing. Some affections (such as love, desire, joy, and gratitude) are exercised toward things that are approved or liked, and others (such as hatred, fear, anger, and grief) are exercised in disapproval or rejection.[38] The affections, then, have objects, that is, what they either approve or reject. What we love, what we fear, in what we rejoice matters greatly for the quality of the affection. True religion exercises the affections toward objects that pertain to the divine: we love God; we hate sin; we hope in the promises of God's Word; we desire to dwell in the house of the Lord. Furthermore, affections propel us into action, so true religion is not simply emotional, but is also practical.[39] In fact, although Edwards values the self-examination that has been commended by other noted theologians, such as Flavel, he says, "Assurance is not to be obtained so much by self-examination, as by action."[40]

True and false joy, then, are distinguished by their objects. The saint, who has true joy, rejoices in God, is pleased and delighted in God and the things of God. From this joy in God springs all their other pleasures and delights. The hypocrite, who has false joy, delights in self and the experience the self is having. The experience itself is what brings happiness and becomes the focus of further experience. True joy takes delight in the perfection and beauty of God. False joy takes delight in an elevated feeling. In true joy, one is so taken up in the enjoyment of the beauty of God that one does not think of oneself and what one has attained. True and false affections, then, lead to different actions. The saint speaks of God, not of her or his own experience. The hypocrite, in contrast, speaks of the experience and the confidence about salvation that comes with it.

37. See Wills, *Inventing America*, 248–49.

38. Edwards, *A Treatise Concerning Religious Affections*, 98.

39. Ibid., 101.

40. Ibid., 195.

In other words, false joy leads to a kind of boasting about one's own condition, whereas true joy leads to praise of God.[41] True happiness, then, is rooted in enjoying the beauty, glory, amiableness, and holiness of God. The saint loves these things for themselves, not for any interest that he or she may have in them.

By linking the affections to the will, happiness is linked to what is pleasing. So Edwards has to explain how the pleasure that the saint takes in God is not in fact based in self-interest. In other words, if one knows that God brings the highest happiness, then would not a desire for God be rooted in a desire for one's own happiness, and so in self-love? Edwards argues that much depends on how one comes to desire God as the highest happiness in the first place. If one first comes to apprehend God's loveliness as it is, then one will be drawn to and desire that loveliness. God's nature itself, not self-interest, awakens the desire.[42] It is only when this love for God is awakened by God's own nature and shows how agreeable enjoyment of God is that a saint will rightly "desire the glorifying and enjoying of God as his happiness."

Earlier in the *Treatise*, Edwards has explained how the saint comes to know the nature of God, which excites this desire. The Spirit of God dwells in the souls of the saints and "communicates himself in his own proper nature." Through this communication, the saint partakes "of God's beauty and Christ's joy."[43] The truly gracious affections of the saints have a spiritual origin, and they acquire a "new inward perception or sensation of their minds," a "spiritual sense" that allows an apprehension of God distinct from anything that would be available simply through natural means.[44] God must make the divine nature known to humans, and even provide the sense through which such knowledge can be perceived. The source of true happiness, then, is God and God alone.

True happiness in God, for Edwards, comes to us from the outside as blessing, and it brings fulfillment. He has retained important concerns about happiness from previous centuries, although he has used

41. Ibid., 249–53.

42. Ibid., 240–41.

43. Ibid., 201.

44. Ibid., 205. The language of the senses, of course, reflects Locke's language for epistemology, but it also reflects John Flavel's language for knowing one's own sincerity. For an account of Puritan influence on Edwards, see Walton, *Jonathan Edwards, Religious Affections*.

the language of his time to express this view of happiness. At the same time, he has also adjusted certain prevailing ideas so that the concerns of the Christian tradition may be preserved. Edwards can talk about the fulfillment that true happiness brings as satisfied desire that is pleasing, but he has been careful to deny that either the desire or the pleasure is rooted in self-interest. The knowledge that brings this happiness is accessible through sense experience, but not experience that comes through the physical senses. God provides the elect with another spiritual sense that allows them to perceive the beauty and holiness of God's nature. Edwards, then, even though he is working with the understanding of happiness in his day as pleasure and satisfied desire, has secured this understanding of happiness within God alone.

By the eighteenth century, happiness could be named as a goal worth pursuing, not only in philosophy, politics, literature, and poetry but also in theology. The way happiness was discussed in larger society shaped the way theological ideas were expressed, but Christians held fast to the idea that the greatest and most secure happiness was to be found in God alone.

As theologians expressed the Christian view of happiness for a new time, some of the language and ideas about that happiness took on new emphases. Concern about desire, and whether it was rightly or wrongly directed, had always had a significant place in Christian theology. As a more positive attitude toward (and greater means for) satisfying desires on earth emerged, language about satisfied desire found a prominent place in talking even about eternal happiness. Also, in keeping with the empiricism of the times, sense experience became the model for how one came to have the knowledge of God that led to true and solid happiness. The need to be able to discern what God was doing in one's own life became great because by providing the key to knowing about one's eternal destiny it also held the key to how happy one could be now in the knowledge of what was yet to come. By stressing satisfied desire, the measure of a happy life was less a matter of external judgment about its praiseworthiness and more a matter of internal experience. The stress on internal testing of one's own heart also contributed to a more internal orientation to happiness.

If the most satisfying and secure happiness could be gained only by sharing in the life of God, then holiness was linked very closely to happiness. Holiness is what made a human being fit to be in God's holy presence, so without it happiness would be compromised. Even though the source of one's holiness was hotly debated (for instance whether one's righteousness was solely imputed by faith, or whether one's obedient works also contributed), it was common for Christians to link happiness and holiness together (Cotton Mather and Matthew Henry were among those who did so).

Just as more ancient theologians had learned from and modified Greek philosophy, theologians in the seventeenth and eighteenth centuries learned from and modified the thinking that was emerging in their time. John Wesley was born into this time of robust concern about happiness, and the topic became important for his way of thinking about salvation. We now turn to his theology in order to draw out a way of thinking about happiness informed both by the deep commitments of Christian theology and by observation of lives of faith in the Methodist movement.

4

John Wesley: Happiness in the Way of Salvation

JOHN WESLEY DID NOT use the word *happiness* in the titles of any of his sermons.[1] The frequency with which he mentions happiness (in more than eighty of his sermons) and the place it occupies in the way of salvation that he commends suggest, though, that the idea has an importance for his thinking that ought to be acknowledged and explored.[2] Since his references to happiness tend to be scattered through his writings rather than appearing in tightly formulated arguments on the subject, it is necessary to draw together his ideas into a sustained description.[3] Such a study shows that he does have a theological understanding of happiness that is closely connected to other concepts central to his theology. This

1. John Wesley did edit and publish in his *Christian Library* "An Enquiry After Happiness" by Richard Lucas. Other works in that collection occasionally mention happiness, but this study will focus on Wesley's original writings as the clearest representations of his own thought.

2. As determined by a word search of *happiness* in *Sermons*, vols. 1–4, edited by Albert C. Outler, of *The Bicentennial Edition of the Works of John Wesley*. A search for related words, such as *cheerful, joy, rejoice,* or *happy* might raise the count. Unless otherwise noted, all references to John Wesley will be cited from *The Bicentennial Edition of the Works of John Wesley* (hereafter *Works*).

3. John Wesley does focus on the nature and ground of Christian joy in Sermon 12, "The Witness of Our Own Spirit," *Works*, 3:299–313, but even this sermon cannot provide by itself a full picture of what he had in mind.

chapter will present an overview of the major ideas about happiness that Wesley held, and the next chapter will explore more thoroughly the connection between happiness and holiness.

MADE FOR HAPPINESS

Since he lived and wrote in the century before Charles Darwin proposed the theory of evolution, John Wesley easily accepted a view of the history of creation that included a literal Adam and Eve in paradise. His understanding of their life before the Fall served as his model for what human life was intended to be. Over his long life and ministry, Wesley continued to develop details about how human nature was hurt with the Fall and how it could be restored to what God intended, but the basic framework remained remarkably stable over time. In a very early sermon "The Image of God," Wesley describes the original image, how it was lost, and what is needed to recover it. He lists four endowments that marked the original image as it was intended to function: (1) human beings imaged God in having understanding that was accurate, clear, could process information quickly, and comprehended many things. (2) Humans also imaged God in having a will that was aligned with God's will because it was filled with love and the affections were ordered properly. (3) Because the understanding and will functioned as they should, the first humans had liberty, that is, they had the freedom to remain as they were because they were not inclined to sin. (4) In this state of proper functioning, human beings were happy; they could fully enjoy the Creator and the creation because they understood things properly and willed what was right.[4] Right understanding, properly functioning will, liberty, and happiness, then, characterized the original image of God as it was supposed to be.[5]

With the Fall, though, each of these endowments was changed. The understanding became clouded, slow, and able to grasp much less, so consequently it was often mistaken. Improperly guided by the understanding, the will came out of alignment with God's will, and in fact, its affections were directed toward things of the world instead of the

---

4. John Wesley, *Works*, 4:293–94. Although this description is given quite early in Wesley's life, a much later sermon describes the original image with the same four endowments, indicating great stability over time in this idea of the image of God for Wesley. See Sermon 62, "The End of Christ's Coming," in *Works*, 3:471–84.

5. Clapper calls peace and happiness "the emotional telos of the entire Christian life," in *John Wesley on Religious Affections*, 87.

things of God. Being controlled by improperly directed affections, the will lost its liberty. Now inclined to sin, it could not direct itself to God as it should. With all this damage to the image of God, human beings lived in misery instead of happiness.[6] The way of salvation is about God's work to undo this damage and its consequences so that humans may once again live in the happiness for which we were made.

This phrase "the happiness for which we were made" is used by Wesley to explain "true religion" (or an authentically lived Christian faith).[7] As we have seen, distinguishing true from false religious practice (or the godly from the ungodly, or sincere holiness from dissimulation) was a major preoccupation of English theologians in this time, and Wesley is no exception. The following summary of true religion comes from a sermon written fairly late in his life, and thus represents his mature theology:

> True religion is right tempers towards God and man. It is, in two words, gratitude and benevolence: gratitude to our Creator and supreme Benefactor, and benevolence to our fellow-creatures. In other words, it is the loving God with all our heart, and our neighbour as ourselves.
>
> It is in consequence of our knowing God loves us that we love him, and love our neighbour as ourselves. Gratitude toward our Creator cannot but produce benevolence to our fellow-creatures. The love of Christ constrains us, not only to be harmless, to do no ill to our neighbour, but to be useful, to be "zealous of good works," "as we have time to do good unto all men," and be patterns to all of true genuine morality, of justice, mercy, and truth. This is religion, and this is happiness, the happiness for which we were made.[8]

In these paragraphs, Wesley clearly indicates that happiness is connected to authentic life with God. That which makes us real Christians is also that which makes us really happy. This connection accounts for why Wesley so often pairs happiness with holiness in his writings.

---

6. John Wesley, *Works*, 4:298–99.

7. The word *religion* here refers only to Christianity and not to the various religions of the world. Wesley is not using this phrase to say that Christianity is true and all others are false. His concern is to distinguish true or real Christianity from a nominal or inauthentic practice of the Christian faith.

8. John Wesley, *Works*, 4:67.

In what follows in that paragraph, Wesley describes the happiness for which we were made:

> This [the happiness for which we were made] begins when we begin to know God, by the teaching of his own Spirit. As soon as the Father of spirits reveals his Son in our hearts, and the Son reveals his Father, the love of God is shed abroad in our hearts; then, and not till then, we are happy. We are happy, first, in the consciousness of his favor, which indeed is better than the life itself; next, in the constant communion with the Father, and with his Son, Jesus Christ; then in all the heavenly tempers which he hath wrought in us by his Spirit; again, in the testimony of his Spirit that all our works please him; and lastly, in the testimony of our own spirit that "in simplicity and godly sincerity we have had our conversation in the world." Standing fast in this liberty from sin and sorrow, wherewith Christ hath made them free, real Christians "rejoice evermore, pray without ceasing, and in everything give thanks." And their happiness still increases as they "grow up into the measure of the stature of the fullness of Christ."[9]

The idea that there is a happiness "for which we were made" suggests that Wesley is concerned about the fulfillment of our natures, as the ancients were.[10] Happiness, for Wesley, is rooted in relationship, and it is this relationship that enables us to be who we were created to be. The way we fulfill our natures and become happy is by right relationship with God that manifests itself through our tempers and works. Love of God and love of neighbor—gratitude and benevolence (wishing well for others)—these are key to happiness. These passages show how central happiness is for Wesley's understanding of true religion, which is also a way of saying it is central for his understanding of salvation.[11] We were made to be happy in God, and salvation is about restoring us to the relationship with God that enables us to be who we were created to be and thus will give us this happiness.

---

9. Ibid.

10. Outler has made this connection when he refers to Wesley as a "eudaemonist." See *Evangelism and Theology in the Wesleyan Spirit*, 127. In the broad sense of meaning that happiness is the end of human life, this characterization is correct, although given the tendency of early Christian theologians to prefer other terms to *eudaimonia*, using this description for Christian theology (including Wesley's) is somewhat misleading.

11. Collins recognizes this point when he notes that Peter Böhler taught Wesley that happiness and holiness are the two fruits of saving faith. See Collins, *John Wesley*, 82.

DESIRE

Although Wesley does not explicitly define the happiness described above in terms of desire, as would be common in his age, desire does play a significant role both in how he understands the human problem and in the restoration of the image of God that brings us true happiness. The way he thinks about desire follows a tradition rooted in Augustine's thinking. Augustine had recognized that happiness is gained when one has what one wants, but he also understood that happiness depends not simply on getting what one wants, but also on wanting the right thing. It is only when one wants that which will truly make one happy that the having it brings real happiness. He distinguished, then, between *cupiditas* and *caritas*, two kinds of love (or two kinds of wanting) that differ, not according to the strength of desire, but according to their objects. *Cupiditas* desires temporal things that can be lost, so the happiness that comes with having those things is insecure. *Caritas*, in contrast, desires eternal things, so happiness found in them is secure.[12] Although both Augustine and Edwards understood that the object of desire makes the crucial difference, Augustine's concern was not to distinguish a true affection from a false one, as Edwards was concerned to do. Rather he was looking for security—yearnings for God would not be disappointed and would bring lasting happiness; but yearnings for anything less than God could not possibly lead to such happiness.

Wesley picks up this idea of misdirected desire at the heart of the human problem in his sermon "Original Sin." There, he identifies three kinds of desire that manifest themselves in the "natural" condition of human beings under the effect of original sin. They belong to a kind of idolatry that Wesley names "love of the world" because through them we "seek happiness in the creature instead of the Creator."[13] These same three desires are discussed even more fully in terms of happiness in his sermon "Spiritual Idolatry." Wesley takes his language for these desires from 1 John 2:15.

The first of these desires Wesley calls the "desire of the flesh," which he describes as "seeking happiness in the gratification of any or all of the external senses; although more particularly of the three lower senses,

Desire distorted

---

12. Babcock, "Cupiditas and Caritas," 1–34.

13. John Wesley, *Works*, 2:179–80.

tasting, smelling, and feeling."[14] This desire need not be confined to "glut-tony, or drunkenness, or shameless debauchery," but may in fact be at work even in someone who is taking ease in retirement. Nor is this form of desire confined to the rich, who have the opportunity of ease and who have the means to buy things for pleasure.[15] The point is not whether the things are "fine" (for instance, delicacies) or "coarse" (for instance, simple bread) but whether these things "make up all the happiness they either have or seek, and usurp the hearts which are due to God."[16] Seeking happiness in these things means valuing the pleasure they bring above all else, or expecting that in having them, one's life is fulfilled, so that one is satisfied with the things rather than looking beyond them to God.

The second desire Wesley names "desire of the eye," which is "seeking happiness in gratifying the imagination (chiefly by means of the eyes)." What Wesley might call the higher senses (sight and hearing) give us access to things that please our imaginations because they are "grand, or beautiful, or uncommon."[17] Works of art, music, fashion, amusements, even study can fall in this category. These things give pleasure that is more mental than physical, but they may become idols for us when we seek our happiness in them. The problem lies not in the things themselves but in one's approach to them. Wesley was himself, for instance, a man of very serious study, and he commended study to his preachers. By including study in this category, he could not mean that study is bad. Rather, the problem would arise if study (or any other of the mental pleasures he lists) displaced God as the source of one's happiness.

One key factor in pleasing the imagination often turns out to be novelty. A thing pleases when it is new in a way it does not once it has become old and familiar. Because of the love of newness, people grow dissatisfied with what they have or what they have experienced and seek the latest thing. There is, then, a kind of restlessness in this desire that drives one beyond enjoying the intrinsic beauty or value of a thing to seeking new pleasure when tired of the old. Following trends and

14. Ibid., 3:106.

15. Although misdirected desire is a problem that cuts across economic class, riches do present a particular danger because they increase one's ability to pursue misdirected desire. See Collins' discussion of the connection between Wesley's cautions about gaining riches and happiness in *John Wesley*, 259.

16. John Wesley, *Works*, 3:106.

17. Ibid., 3:106.

having or experiencing the latest thing, then, becomes more important even than the objects or activities themselves. Again, it may be easier for people of means to pursue and fulfill this desire, but less wealthy folk may also take undue pleasure in grand, beautiful, uncommon, or new things.

Wesley calls the third desire the "pride of life," which means "seeking happiness in the praise of men, which above all things engenders pride."[18] At its heart, this desire is for honor and status. Wesley acknowledges that a good reputation is to be valued, but once again, the problem lies not simply in what others think, but in seeking happiness in what others think. Not only the desire for praise, but also the avoidance of disparagement can drive one's thoughts and actions. Whether seeking favorable attention or avoiding unfavorable attention, one makes other human beings, instead of God, the standard by which one operates. Once more, this desire is not restricted to the rich. Having money may enable a person to rise in status, but a person does not need a lot of money in order to seek high esteem from others.

In an age that so clearly linked happiness with gratified desire and that was so clearly engaged in the pursuit of happiness, Wesley offered an account of the ways that gratified desire can displace God in our lives. He frames his criticism in terms of idolatry rather than (as Augustine did) in terms of security, but the problem of misdirected desire is clearly fundamental for him to the question of happiness.[19] At the center of each of the desires he names is loving some creature more than the Creator. And only love for the Creator above all else will bring true happiness. In the companion sermon to "Spiritual Idolatry," entitled "Spiritual Worship," Wesley makes the point this way: "In this alone can you find the happiness you seek—in the union of your spirit with the Father of spirits: in the knowledge and love of him who is the fountain of happiness sufficient for all the souls he has made."[20]

18. Ibid., 3:109.

19. Collins's work suggests that Wesley's concern about idolatry may have shared Augustine's concern about security to some extent. He points out how Wesley's cautions about riches were rooted in "setting one's heart on the ephemeral and fleeting, that is, on anything less than God." To seek happiness in things that are less than God is to seek happiness in things that will not last, as Augustine knew. See *John Wesley: A Theological Journey*, 259.

20. John Wesley, *Works*, 3:101.

HAPPINESS AND SALVATION

Misdirected desire, for Wesley, is a manifestation of the damage done to the image of God, and so it is linked to original sin. We were made to be happy, but with our wills out of alignment with God's will (and so our desires directed to lesser things), we cannot help but be miserable in the most profound sense. Certainly, some temporary and superficial happiness is possible through gratifying desires for things of the world, but those things do not satisfy our deepest need for relationship with God, and the desire for them leads us further away from the relationship that will truly satisfy. Wesley takes this problem to be universal, and he also understands it to be a problem that we cannot overcome by ourselves.[21] Wesley has put the question of happiness right at the heart of the need for salvation.

Since happiness is rooted in relationship with God, regaining that relationship is essential. Wesley describes how such happiness begins, in "Spiritual Worship":

> This eternal life then commences when it pleases the Father to reveal his Son in our hearts; when we first know Christ, being enabled to "call him Lord by the Holy Ghost"; when we can testify, our conscience bearing us witness in the Holy Ghost, "the life which I now live, I live by faith in the Son of God, who loved me, and gave himself for me." And then it is that happiness begins—happiness real, solid, substantial. Then it is that heaven is opened in the soul, that the proper, heavenly state commences, while the love of God, as loving us, is shed abroad in the heart, instantly producing love to all mankind: general, pure benevolence, together with its genuine fruits, lowliness, meekness, patience, contentedness in every state; an entire, clear, full acquiescence in the whole will of God, enabling us to "rejoice evermore, and in everything to give thanks."[22]

This passage echoes the description quoted above in which Wesley described the happiness for which we were made. God takes the gracious initiative to make something known to us, which we embrace by faith, and in doing so, we gain a consciousness both of God's favor (in the previous passage) and of our new life because of that favor (in this passage). Wesley's description of the beginning of happiness calls to mind

21. Ibid., 2:170–85.
22. Ibid., 3:96.

justification (consciousness of God's favor), and the witness of God's Spirit with one's own spirit to being a child of God. Because love of God produces love of neighbor and heavenly tempers, which are grounds for rejoicing, Wesley links happiness to sanctification as well. As Wesley makes clear through repeated pairing of these terms, happiness and holiness belong together. Theologically, for Wesley, happiness belongs right at the center of his understanding of how God saves human beings. Gaining right relationship with God in justification leads directly to new life and to new relationships with others. Love of God and love of neighbor—gratitude and benevolence—which characterize true religion and come through God's saving work in human life, mark the beginning of true happiness.

Wesley's understanding of happiness includes a cognitive dimen- sion. There is a kind of knowing that leads to happiness—knowing God's love, knowing one's life to bear the fruit of being in loving relationship with God. This knowledge is cause for rejoicing, and like Edwards, Wesley adopts language of an inner "sense" experience to explain how this knowledge is gained. Wesley connects the new birth that marks the beginning of the real renewal of the image of God in one's life to the activating of spiritual senses.[23] Through an inner seeing, hearing, tasting, and feeling, a person becomes aware of grace and the change that grace is effecting. At the same time, a person becomes aware of peace, joy, and love. So the renewal of the image of God brings the happiness that was lost when that image was damaged.[24] This renewal involves a cognitive reorientation to God, to oneself, and to the world, so true happiness will have an element of new understanding.[25]

Justification and new birth in Wesley's way of salvation are closely connected, then, to his understanding of happiness. They mark the beginning of true happiness, just as they mark the beginning of right relationship with God and the renewal of the image of God. For Wesley, salvation did not refer simply to one's ultimate destiny with God after death. He is careful to specify in one seminal sermon that "the salvation

23. For a discussion of how Wesley's use of spiritual senses helped him hold together an empiricist framework for epistemology with a Platonic understanding of access to a special realm of knowledge, see Miles, "Instrumental Role of Reason," 77–106.

24. John Wesley, *Works*, 2:192–94; see also 4:168–76.

25. Randy Maddox suggests that the "crucial dimension" of happiness is the self-acceptance that comes with being in right relationship with God and others. See *Responsible Grace*, 287 n. 24.

which is here spoken of is not what is frequently understood by that word, the going to heaven, eternal happiness." "Going to heaven" is not being ruled out, but Wesley is expanding the idea of salvation to include the whole scope of the work of God in one's life. It is particularly characteristic of Wesley's soteriology that he thought of salvation as "a present thing, a blessing which, through the free mercy of God, ye are now in possession of."[26] If salvation is a present thing, then the happiness that accompanies it is also a present thing. One does not have to wait until after death to be happy in God. Such happiness is available to a person now.

PLEASURE

In an age in which pleasure was often taken to bring happiness, Wesley had to address the way the two might be related. His own framework for talking about happiness pressed for resolution: If, on the one hand, happiness is a present thing, and happiness in the present is constituted by pleasure, then could receiving pleasure from gratifying desires of the flesh, of the eye, and of praise really be the problem that Wesley has described? If on the other hand, gratifying these desires is indeed a problem, does pleasure have any place in a Christian's life?

Wesley takes up this question directly when he replies to objections about his doctrine of perfection. A Christian who has been made perfect in love of God and love of neighbor would be a Christian whose will had been realigned with God's will. Desire would no longer be misdirected in the three ways noted above. Would this mean, then, that a real Christian would be completely indifferent as to what might be pleasing? Or perhaps would having a preference for pleasing things indicate that a person was not yet fully perfected in love? Wesley takes up this matter in *A Plain Account of Christian Perfection*. He poses the question and gives an answer in this way:

> Q. *But can any one who has a pure heart prefer pleasing to unpleasing food; or use any pleasure of sense which is not strictly necessary? If so, how do they differ from others?*

> A. The difference between these and others in taking pleasant food is, (1.) They need none of these things to make them happy; for they have a spring of happiness within. They see and love God. Hence they rejoice evermore, and in everything give thanks.

26. John Wesley, *Works*, 2:156.

(2.) They may use them, but they do not seek them. (3.) They use them sparingly, and not for the sake of the thing itself. This being premised, we answer directly,—Such a one may use pleasing food, without the danger which attends those who are not saved from sin. He may prefer it to unpleasing, though equally wholesome, food, as a means of increasing thankfulness, with a single eye to God, who giveth us all things richly to enjoy: On the same principle, he may smell to a flower, or eat a bunch of grapes, or take any other pleasure which does not lessen but increase his delight in God. Therefore, neither can we say that one perfected in love would be incapable of marriage, and of worldly business: If he were called thereto, he would be more capable than ever; as being able to do all things without hurry or carefulness, without any distraction of spirit.[27]

The point of this exchange seems to be that pleasure of itself is not the problem. God has given us a world to enjoy, and as long as we enjoy it without allowing it to displace God as the center and source of our happiness, then we are actually living as humans were intended to live. Wesley had described the happiness of Adam and Eve before the Fall in this way: "to live was to enjoy . . . at full liberty to enjoy either the Creator or the creation; to indulge in rivers of pleasure, ever new, ever pure from any mixture of pain."[28] So God's original intent for us was pleasure, and it is precisely by being made perfect in love that we regain that original possibility of being able to take appropriate pleasure in the world, rather than being distracted by it away from God.

We have already seen how Wesley qualified the desire of the eye and the desire of praise to some extent. The problem did not lie in beauty itself, or in study itself, or in having a good reputation. The problem was in seeking happiness through these things. Now Wesley has made the same point with regard to the desire of the flesh. Not even the pleasures of the senses are in and of themselves bad. The problem lies in seeking happiness through them. In other words, when we count on these things to fulfill us, or when their lack or loss has the power to make us miserable, then they have displaced God as the source and center of our happiness. The human problem is that we are inclined to let them displace God in this way, and what God's gracious activity in our lives accomplishes is to defeat the power of that inclination so that we may

27. John Wesley, *A Plain Account of Christian Perfection*, 58–59.
28. John Wesley, *Works*, 4:295.

give God the proper place in our hearts and lives. When that happens, we may take genuine pleasure in creation as the gift of God for our enjoyment. Just as it was for Augustine, for Wesley learning to desire well was essential to happiness.

The cognitive dimension of the renewal of the image of God matters for the ability to take appropriate pleasure in the world. Understanding God's love in such a way as to be in right relationship with God, knowing oneself to be changed by that relationship and seeing the fruits of that change in one's own life, understanding the things of the world as God's gifts, and seeing other people as loved by God and so deserving of our own love and good will—all these provide for us an orientation to our surroundings that allow us to value and treat ourselves, each other, and the world as God wants us to. Understanding these things properly enables us to enjoy them properly. We can, then, take pleasure in seeing ourselves grow in those characteristics and dispositions that demonstrate God's work in us, or in grateful use of the gifts of creation, or in contributing positively to the work of God in the lives of our neighbors. All these may become occasions of happiness for us because God is the source and center of the pleasure that they bring.

THE FEELING OF HAPPINESS

In chapter 3, I noted that eighteenth-century theologians did not distinguish between the words *happiness* and *joy* in the way that many Christians today do. Wesley was aware of the need to distinguish a superficial good feeling from genuine happiness, but he used different words to do so.[29] Several times, Wesley warns against "levity," which he can contrast with "seriousness." When Wesley cautions against levity, he has in mind diversion and amusement that do not edify the person or bring glory to God. He is also concerned about hurtful humor, in other words, joking at another person's expense. "Seriousness" points to engagement in behavior that does edify or bring glory to God.[30] Such seriousness is not the opposite of true happiness, it is instead the opposite

29. In the field of psychology, the study of emotion is currently of great interest, and definitions of the language of emotion can vary according to the researcher. When I use the word *feeling* here, I do not have in mind any particular technical, psychological definition of this word. I intend it to signal a relatively brief, conscious, internal, subjective state—what ordinary people mean when they say "I feel good" or "I feel bad."

30. See John Wesley's journal reflection on his inner feeling, *Works*, 18:209.

of a rather insubstantial feeling that accompanies behavior that does no good and may do harm. Wesley can also distinguish being "happy" from being "merry." He says:

> A glutton, a drunkard, a gamester may be "merry"; but he cannot be happy. The beau, the belle, may eat and drink, and rise up to play; but they still feel they are not happy. Men or women may adorn their own dear persons with all the colours of the rainbow. They may dance and sing, and hurry to and fro, and flutter hither and thither. They may roll up and down in their splendid carriages and talk insipidly to each other. They may hasten from one diversion to another; but happiness is not there.[31]

Amusement is not real happiness. Having a particularly "merry," temporary mood is not real happiness.[32] This kind of feeling can come and go, and in fact it takes continued diversion to maintain it. It can all too easily become boredom when novelty fades.

The kind of happiness that Wesley commends is, of course, a feeling in some sense, but this feeling has a different character than temporary mood elevation. In Wesley's time, the language of what we would now call emotions was changing, and his most substantive discussion of the inner life more often used the language of affections, tempers, and passions than feelings.[33] He did use the language of feeling occasionally, but not with enough precision or frequency to provide a truly useful definition. Nor did he often use the word "feel" or "feeling" when he spoke about happiness. In contrast, we do ordinarily talk about happiness as a feeling, so what can we say about Wesley's understanding that connects with the kind of experience we mean when we talk about feeling?

The work of two scholars sheds some light on what it might mean to talk about happiness as a feeling for Wesley. Gregory Clapper draws attention to the way Wesley uses the word *feel* for matters of the heart in comparison to the physical sense of touch. We have already seen in the discussion on desire above that Wesley thought of "higher" and "lower" physical senses. Touch or feeling was the lowest of all. Similarly, Wesley

---

31. John Wesley, *Works*, 3:99.

32. When I use the word *mood* I am not intending any technical, psychological definition of the word. I am using it in its colloquial meaning, as an internal, subjective state that people often refer to as "good" or "bad." The usage section of *American Heritage Dictionary of the English Language* refers to it as a state of mind or feeling.

33. I will cover what he meant by these terms in the next chapter.

can refer to feeling as the lowest knowledge of God. Clapper defines feeling as "conscious sensation" analogous to the sensation of touch, an immediate but ephemeral experience.[34] Theodore Runyon gives feeling more importance. He notes an instance in a letter where Wesley defines "feeling" as "being inwardly conscious of," and Runyon explains that when Wesley uses "feeling" for religious experience, he has in mind a sensation that is received through the spiritual senses rather than the physical senses, and this sensation occurs because the Holy Spirit is communicating with us.[35] Just as bodily sensations have to be interpreted to deliver knowledge, spiritual sensations also have to be interpreted. But spiritual sensations, the feelings of the heart, provide the input of the Holy Spirit's communication. They may be "low" in the sense of basic and by themselves incomplete because they still need interpretation, but they are vital to grasping God's love for us.

Both Clapper and Runyon describe feeling as some kind of conscious awareness. So if we feel happy in God, what are we aware of? To utilize Runyon's explanation, we would be inwardly conscious of a communication of the Holy Spirit that conveys God's love and so produces what Wesley describes as "calm, humble rejoicing."[36] Wesley also frequently connects happiness with peace, the kind of peace that "banishes all doubt, all painful uncertainty," just as it "banishes fear," specifically any uncertainty or fear about one's status before and relationship to God.[37] Happiness is a state of mind, but it is state of mind grounded in the blessing of grace. It is certainly pleasant, but unlike levity, it is not based on pleasure from created things. It is a feeling that comes with knowing one's security in God. This happiness does not depend on circumstances (attending a party, getting attention, acquiring a new item of clothing) as mood elevation does. It is steady and sure across all

---

34. Clapper, *John Wesley on Religious Affections*, 60–62.

35. Runyon, *New Creation*, 152.

36. John Wesley, *Works*, 1:223.

37. Ibid. Collins takes the peace and joy that constitute happiness to come from a sense of forgiveness, see *John Wesley*, 82, and *A Real Christian*, 57. This sense of forgiveness is certainly the beginning of happiness for Wesley, but I do not think it is the entirety of it. Because Wesley can also link happiness to the awareness of the fruits of the Spirit in one's life, it would seem that one is happy not just in having been forgiven but also in becoming the person God wants one to be. There could well be peace and calm and humility associated with that aspect of one's relationship with God.

circumstances because it is anchored in relationship with God, whose transcendence and immanence cut across all circumstances.[38]

Charles Wesley expresses this kind of happiness well in his hymn "Thou Hidden Source of Calm Repose":

> Thou hidden source of calm repose,
> thou all-sufficient love divine,
> my help and refuge from my foes,
> secure I am if thou art mine;
> and lo! from sin and grief and shame
> I hide me, Jesus, in thy name.
>
> Thy mighty name salvation is,
> and keeps my happy soul above,
> comfort it brings, and power and peace,
> and joy and everlasting love;
> to me with thy dear name are given
> pardon and holiness and heaven.
>
> Jesus, my all in all thou art,
> my rest in toil, my ease in pain,
> the healing of my broken heart,
> in war my peace, in loss my gain,
> my smile beneath the tyrant's frown,
> in shame my glory and my crown.
>
> In want my plentiful supply,
> in weakness my almighty power,
> in bonds my perfect liberty,
> my light in Satan's darkest hour,
> in grief my joy unspeakable,
> my life in death, my heaven in hell.[39]

Jesus is the source of calm, comfort, and security for the "happy soul," even through the difficult circumstances expressed in verses 3 and 4.

John Wesley understood this happiness to be so central to Christian faith that he even claimed, "that every Christian is happy, and that he who is not happy is not a Christian."[40] He can only make this claim

38. Clapper points out that all of the religious affections should have this enduring quality because they indicate a "general orientation" to life more than ephemeral feelings, in *John Wesley on Religious Affections*, 51–53, 120.

39. Charles Wesley, "Thou Hidden Source of Calm Repose," verses 1–4. All hymns were accessed from Charles Wesley's Published Verse, Duke Center for Studies in the Wesleyan Tradition.

40. John Wesley, *Works*, 3:100. For how he qualifies this statement, see chapter 6.

because he has distinguished "merry" from "happy." He would not say that every Christian is merry or that one who is not merry is not a Christian. Happiness, as we shall see in subsequent chapters, is about much more than feeling, even if it includes feeling.

THE HAPPINESS OF ALL CREATION

So far, what we have seen of Wesley's understanding of happiness has centered on human beings, but he actually has a very broad view of the happiness God intends: "The great Creator made nothing to be miserable, but every creature to be happy in its kind. And upon a general review of the works of his hands he pronounced them all "very good"; which they would not have been had not every intelligent creature—yea, everyone capable of pleasure and pain—been happy in answering the end of its creation."[41] Not simply human beings, but all creation was made for happiness. All creation is happy when it is fulfilling God's intent for it. In fact, the happiness of God's creatures bears testimony to God:

> Now the wisdom, as well as the power of God, is abundantly manifested in his creation, in the formation and arrangement of all his works, in heaven above and in the earth beneath; and in adapting them all to the several ends for which they were designed; insomuch that each of them apart from the rest is good, but all together are very good; all conspiring together in one connected system, to the glory of God in the happiness of his intelligent creatures.[42]

Happiness, then, far from being restricted to human beings is intended for all that God has made as each creature attains the end for which it was created.

Sadly, the happiness of all creation was compromised in the Fall. Wesley accepts the view that although human beings were the ones who turned away from God's intent for them, the consequences of that turning away extended to all creation. He says: "And then it was that 'the creature,' every creature, 'was subject to vanity,' to sorrow, to pain of every kind, to all manner of evils."[43]

But if the whole creation shares in the misery of the Fall, it will also share in the restoration that God intends to bring about through Jesus

41. Ibid.
42. Ibid., 2:552.
43. Ibid., 2:442.

Christ. Wesley envisions a new creation in which each element retains its nature (so it can meet its end) without destroying other things. So fire will heat without consuming fuel, earth will produce fruits for nourishment but not thorns or poisonous plants, animals will live without preying on other animals. In the new creation, there will be nothing to give any creature "uneasiness," so "when God has 'renewed the face of the earth,' and their corruptible body has put on incorruption, they shall enjoy happiness suited to their state, without alloy, without interruption, and without end."[44]

John Wesley's understanding of happiness pervades his theology. From his doctrine of creation to his doctrine of eschatology, God's purpose for all things culminates in happiness. For human beings, happiness has a central place in soteriology. Both the nature of the human problem and its correction are explained in terms of happiness. By highlighting this idea, Wesley is accepting a high value of his time, but he is not doing so uncritically. His reflection on desire shows engagement with but not simple acceptance of the ideas of his time. He has found in the Christian tradition resources that deepen and guide the pursuit of happiness of his age.

Because happiness is so centrally linked to salvation in his theology, it is also paired with holiness. The authenticity of one's life as a Christian grounds the happiness that one gains as a Christian. It is to this pairing of happiness with holiness that we now turn.

44. Ibid., 2:447.

5

John Wesley: Happiness through Holiness

IN HIS INTRODUCTION TO the critical edition of Wesley's sermons,
Albert C. Outler calls holiness and happiness "correlates."[1] In another
work, Outler points out, "We have fifty-four quotes where Wesley explicitly pairs off 'happy and holy' (or vice versa) and the correlation is
constant throughout his works and career."[2] Indeed, they are so often
paired together that it is evident they should be mutually illuminating.
In actual practice in the study of the Wesleyan tradition, though, reflection on holiness has taken precedence over reflection on happiness
(the indices and titles of books in Wesleyan Studies bear witness to the
relative attention paid to each idea). This chapter attempts to display the
correlation between these two terms in order to show the essential connection between happiness and holiness. In the Wesleyan tradition, it is
precisely through holiness that true happiness is gained.

FITTING WITH GOD'S PURPOSE

To begin to explore the connection between happiness and holiness, I
want to draw on a meaning of the word *happy* that was used more in the
eighteenth century than in our time. Even if Wesley did not consciously

1. Outler, "Introduction," 1:35.
2. Outler, *Evangelism and Theology in the Wesleyan Spirit*, 129.

intend this meaning when he wrote, it helps illumine the connection between the two ideas that were so important to him. This old use of the word *happy* conveys the idea that something is fit, suitable, and appropriate. A "happy thought" or "happy use of language" indicates a sentiment or phrase particularly suited to the occasion. A home is "happily situated" when it is well placed in its surroundings. Wesley does not explicitly make use of this definition when he talks about happiness, but it seems clear in his theology that a life that corresponds to the structure of existence as God has created it to be is in this sense "happy"—in other words, it would be a life appropriately lived.

We have already seen how a major motivation for living a life of holiness in seventeenth- and eighteenth-century England lay in the desire to be fit for relationship with God. God is holy, so those who share in God's life must also be holy. Living appropriately and authentically according to our natures and according to God's will for us makes us suitable participants in relationship with God. There is also personal satisfaction in knowing one's proper place in the way things ought to be and living appropriately. Happiness is, then, both "objective" in the sense that there is something outside the individual to which the individual's life needs to "fit," and it is also "subjective" in the sense that the individual feels fulfilled by the fitting. That "fit" is, of course, enabled by God's grace, not merely the result of human effort, but in responding to that grace we are living according to God's desire for us.[3] When our desires "fit" with God's desires, we live in the wholeness that salvation brings.

HOLINESS OF HEART

At times, Wesley could use "holiness" and "Christian perfection" as synonyms.[4] By either name, the essence is love. The goal of Christian life, which corresponds to the end of human nature itself, is to love God and neighbor.[5] Wesley frequently distinguished two aspects of holiness, inward and outward. He also specified a direction from one to the other—inward holiness gave rise to outward holiness. Maintaining this direction was important because it also maintained the priority of God's

3. The roles of grace and human action in Wesley's theology have been explained in many resources. See especially Maddox, *Responsible Grace*.

4. John Wesley, *Works*, 2:104.

5. Outler calls this dual love "the essence of 'holiness'" for Wesley. See Outler, "Introduction," 1:35.

grace in making us holy. Grace enables us to love, and then our actions follow from that love.

We have seen in the previous chapter how misdirected desire lies at the heart of the human problem in Wesley's theology. The correction that is needed, then, is for love to be properly directed. This redirecting of desire is one component of what Wesley sometimes called the "religion of the heart."[6] By using the word "heart," Wesley of course was speaking metaphorically to express a dimension of human life that had a central role in his understanding of Christian faith. This dimension can be thought of as "deep" or "inward" because it lies behind conscious thoughts and deliberate actions as the orientation or motivation that gives rise to them. It includes but encompasses more than "feeling" because it names not simply what most people think of as emotions but also the will and its inclinations.[7] Desire belongs to this dimension because it directs our attention in the world. We pay attention to the things we want, and then usually our actions are directed to gaining what we want. Desire, then, is the deep background for what we think and do. The fundamental healing that we need must take place at this deep level before our conscious thoughts and deliberate actions may be properly directed.

Human beings depend on God for this healing. God is love, so loving as God loves is essential to the renewal of the image of God in us. In Wesley's understanding of salvation, God displays God's love for us in such a powerful way that it awakens our love for God in return.[8] Because grace initiates this healing, the happiness that ultimately results from it is a blessing—grounded in a gift from God. When we love God, we will also love—as God does—those things that God has created. Fitting our desires with God's desires means learning to love as God loves. To gain true happiness, desires need not just to be satisfied, they also need to be shaped to want what is truly good. Only when they have been rightly directed will their satisfaction bring true happiness. This

---

6. This phrase appears in several sermons. See, for instance, "The Way to the Kingdom," John Wesley, *Works*, 1:221.

7. For a discussion of Wesley's use of "heart," see Maddox, "A Change of Affections," 3–31.

8. The effects of God's display of love are explained well in "The Witness of the Spirit, Discourses I and II," in John Wesley, *Works*, 1:267–98. For a description that explicitly links this witness to happiness, see "An Israelite Indeed," in ibid., 3:283.

love is so important for happiness that Wesley can say, "And according to the degree of our love is the degree of our happiness."[9]

Although it is central and irreplaceable, love is only one word that can be used to describe holiness of heart. The word "heart" for Wesley encompassed a cluster of ideas that included the affections and the tempers. His call to holiness of heart was often specifically directed to a change in tempers.[10] Wesley scholars have not agreed on whether or not the words "affections" and "tempers" have a consistently different reference in Wesley's writing.[11] Apart from the precise use of terminology, though, they do seem to agree that Wesley distinguishes relatively stable from relatively transient affective states—and holiness of heart concerns both. Regarding the former, the concern is with an enduring disposition that marks one's character. In modern English, we might refer to a person's temperament to convey this idea. A person could be usually calm and easy-going, or to the contrary, excitable or easy to anger. These stable dispositions are distinct from, but give rise to, more transient affective reactions to specific circumstances. For instance, a person who is characteristically patient will respond differently to an unexpected delay than someone who is characteristically impatient. The feeling displayed in the moment (from the patient disposition, a calm reaction; and from the impatient disposition, an angry one) arises from and reflects the deep disposition. The more transient responses are specifically directed toward some object, while the stable disposition is a general orientation.

Wesley used the word "passions" to talk about some transient responses to objects. Typically, if he understood the responsiveness as positive, he called it an "affection" and if he understood it as negative he used the word "passion." The former expressed a governed and ordered love, whereas the latter was taken to be ungoverned.[12] In other words, with passion our desires have control of us, but with affections we are controlling and properly directing our desires.

9. Ibid., 3:283.

10. Maddox, "A Change of Affections," 14–17.

11. Clapper takes "temper" and "affection" as interchangeable, while Maddox distinguishes them. See Clapper, *John Wesley on Religious Affections*, 53, and Maddox, "A Change of Affections," 15. For more on the use of these terms, see Clapper, "John Wesley's Language of the Heart," 94–102.

12. Clapper, *John Wesley on Religious Affections*, 54–55. In making this distinction, Wesley was in line with the usage of many in his age. See Dixon, *From Passions to Emotions*, 62.

For Wesley, the wholeness of salvation must begin in the heart, and he shows how holiness of heart fits in the way of salvation. He describes new birth as a change in the soul "from inward sinfulness to inward holiness." The creature's love becomes conformed to the Creator's love, so "Earthly desires, the desire of the flesh, the desire of the eyes, and the pride of life, are in that instant changed by the mighty power of God into heavenly desires." This change in desire, then, expresses itself in the affections and passions: "Pride and haughtiness subside into lowliness of heart; as does anger, with all turbulent and unruly passions, into calmness, meekness, and gentleness. In a word, the earthly, sensual, devilish mind gives place to 'the mind that was in Christ Jesus.'"[13]

As this quotation shows, a change in "heart" involves also a change in "mind." The tendency since the eighteenth century has been to distinguish reason and emotion quite sharply, sometimes expressed in opposing "head" and "heart."[14] Recently, though, a growing body of literature in the study of emotion has shown that some cognitive understanding is an essential ingredient to emotional responses.[15] Affections and passions are responses to something. They are directed to some object, and they arise because of how that object is understood. One is not simply angry, one is angry *about* something. Being angry *about* involves some understanding of the person or situation toward which anger is directed, such as understanding oneself to be slighted or understanding an action to be unjust. Those understandings in turn depend on expectations and values that are held by one's social community, for instance, what kind of respect is due to oneself or what constitutes justice. If cognition is not just conscious thought process (or logical reasoning) but includes understanding of the world (or a world view), then emotional responses to what goes on in the world cannot help but be shaped by one's understanding of it. Emotion and cognition are more closely related than is often commonly acknowledged.

Even without having recently developed theories of emotion at his disposal, Wesley's theology displays the insight explored in the previous

13. John Wesley, *Works*, 3:174.

14. For an account of the historical shift that created the overarching category "emotion" and opposed it to reason and will, see Dixon, *From Passions to Emotions*.

15. For some orientation to the study of emotion in cognitive psychology and cultural anthropology, see Reddy, *Navigation of Feeling*. Reddy himself speaks of emotions as "goal-activations of thought material," 128.

chapter that a changed understanding provides the foundation for changed desire, which in turn will allow changed tempers and affections. Understanding oneself to be a child of God changes one's basic orientation toward self and others and opens the possibility of loving as God loves. Seeing others as God sees them enables us to love them as God loves them, and therefore we may respond to them differently. When Wesley explains what it means to love neighbor, he says: "to bear them real goodwill; to desire their happiness as sincerely as we desire the happiness of our own souls; yea, we are in a sense to honour them (seeing we are directed by the Apostle to 'honour all men') as the creatures of God; nay, as immortal spirits who are capable of knowing, of loving, and of enjoying him to all eternity. We are to honour them as redeemed by his blood who 'tasted death for every man.'"[16] To see another as the valued creature of God is a cognitive shift that allows an emotional shift. For instance, an action by another person that might normally produce anger might be understood instead as a consequence of human frailty with which one can empathize and forgive; or an economic situation that previously just seemed to be "the way of things" might be understood as oppression because it harms people whom God loves, so instead of passively accepting it, a person may feel distressed and so moved to resist it. Learning to love as God loves, including seeing the world as God sees it, belongs to the process of sanctification in Wesley's theology.

The process begins with justification and new birth, and it ends with entire sanctification. Between these two points, Wesley acknowledged that a person's love, and therefore a person's holiness, might be "*mixed*. He [a person born again but not yet entirely sanctified] was humble, but not entirely; his humility was mixed with pride. He was meek, but his meekness was frequently interrupted by anger, or some uneasy and turbulent passion." As long as love of God is mixed with love of creature (in the idolatrous sense, and not as God loves creatures), then a person is vulnerable to doubt and fear that can unsettle holy affections. The hope, though, is for complete change of heart that is filled completely with love of God and neighbor. And with this change that brings uninterrupted love, a person gains "continual joy in the Lord."[17]

The degree of happiness that a Christian can expect to enjoy depends directly on the degree of holiness of heart. This side of perfection,

16. John Wesley, *Works*, 3:130.
17. Ibid., 3:176.

then, happiness will be as mixed as holiness is, and the pursuit of happiness is linked to the pursuit of holiness. If we are happy when our lives fit with God's intention, then the more completely we conform to the mind of Christ, the happier we will be.

HOLINESS OF LIFE

The renewal of the image of God may be something that happens "inwardly," but Wesley always maintained that inward love had to show itself in outward works. The "root of religion" may lie in the heart, but "it cannot but put forth branches."[18] Outler describes Wesley's understanding of holiness as "active love." More than a feeling, love is acted out in concrete ways toward one's neighbor.[19] What begins as inward, if it is genuine, cannot help but be expressed outwardly. Wesley is equally clear, though, that outward action that "has no root in the heart, is nothing worth."[20] Holiness is not complete unless it is both inward and outward. For this reason, Wesley urged Methodists to pursue holiness of heart *and* life.

If holiness of heart begins in love of God, it extends to love of others precisely as a way of loving God. Wesley ponders the command to love God with *all* one's heart:

> Not that we are to love or delight in none but him [God]. For he hath commanded us not only to love our neighbour—that is, all men—as ourselves; to desire and pursue their happiness as sincerely and steadily as our own; but also to love many of his creatures in the strictest sense—to delight in them, to enjoy them—only in such a manner and measure as we know and feel

18. Ibid., 1:541.

19. Outler, "Introduction," 1:223 n. 31. Outler also says in this note that active love yields happiness as a "by-product." This choice of language seems to me to be misleading. Although it is true that one should not do something for another simply for the good feeling that one gets from such an action, the happiness of which Wesley speaks is much more than a by-product (or side effect) of holiness. It is the end or goal of human existence, and a central insight in learning to love as God loves is that another's happiness matters as much as one's own. So holiness through works of mercy aims directly at enabling happiness for another. In addition, the happiness gained for oneself through holiness of life, while perhaps not the primary motive for action, is central to the experience of present salvation. In neither case is "by-product" the best way to express what is going on.

20. John Wesley, *Works*, 1:542.

not to indispose but to prepare us for the enjoyment of him. Thus, then, we are called to love God with all our heart.[21]

As we have seen before, love and happiness are tied together. Love, Wesley points out here, in its strict meaning consists in delighting in and enjoying another. We are primarily to delight in and enjoy God, but we cannot do so without also delighting in and enjoying God's creatures—not in a way that competes with enjoyment of God, but rather in a way that encourages and enriches enjoyment of God. In this way, one's own happiness is linked to the happiness of others. When one desires and pursues another person's happiness as much as one's own, it is possible to delight in and enjoy that person's happiness. Rejoicing in seeing another of God's beloved creatures thrive enriches one's own happiness. By acting out of love to increase another's happiness, one's own happiness (in the love of God) becomes a blessing to the other. And by delighting in the happiness of another, the other's happiness becomes a blessing to oneself. In this way of thinking, the "pursuit of happiness" is not simply one's own private, individual concern; it also encompasses pursuing happiness on behalf of others as well. The desire for another's happiness (inward holiness) leads to activity that contributes to another's happiness (outward holiness).[22]

Happiness and active love (holiness) belong together so fully that they constitute "true religion." Another look at a passage considered in chapter 4 shows the connection:

> True religion is right tempers towards God and man. It is, in two words, gratitude and benevolence: gratitude to our Creator and supreme Benefactor, and benevolence to our fellow-creatures. In other words, it is the loving God with all our heart, and our neighbour as ourselves.
>
> It is in consequence of our knowing God loves us that we love him, and love our neighbour as ourselves. Gratitude toward our

---

21. Ibid., 4:383.

22. I differ from Outler in the way I understand the difference between "inward" and "outward" holiness. In several places, Outler identifies inward holiness as love of God and outward holiness as love of neighbor (see for instance *Works*, 1:426 n. 66). It seems to me, though, that "inward" ought to refer to the "heart," with its tempers and affections. There are right tempers and affections toward neighbor as well as toward God, just as there are outward works that express love toward God as well as outward works that express love toward neighbor—thus the need for works of piety as well as works of mercy.

Creator cannot but produce benevolence to our fellow-creatures. The love of Christ constrains us, not only to be harmless, to do no ill to our neighbour, but to be useful, to be "zealous of good works," "as we have time to do good unto all men," and be patterns to all of true genuine morality, of justice, mercy, and truth. This is religion, and this is happiness, the happiness for which we were made.[23]

True religion, then begins in the heart as right tempers, which are named here specifically as gratitude and benevolence. A rightly tempered heart will be characteristically grateful to God and will characteristically want good for others. This true religion constitutes our happiness because through it we are conforming to the design God has for humanity. Notice that for Wesley "benevolence" does not mean simply thinking about good things for others; it means actively engaging in doing good for them, that is, in promoting their well-being, or one could say, pursuing their happiness.

Wesley makes clear that although giving one's whole heart to God "is the truest happiness, indeed the only true happiness which is to be found under the sun," this love will express itself through action rather than inaction. Anyone who loves God will want to use every opportunity to converse with God, so performing works of piety (such as prayer and searching Scripture) serve as "means of increasing the love from which they spring; and of consequence they increase our happiness in the same proportion." So also performing works of mercy (such as feeding the hungry or visiting the sick) because of love for God and neighbor brings pleasure that does "immensely increase our happiness."[24] The happiness for which we were made, then, needs "doing" to be fully realized.

Wesley's thirteen discourses on the Sermon on the Mount explore the "doing" that follows from genuine faith. The first three of these discourses focus on the Beatitudes, and Wesley notes in these sermons that the Greek word beginning each of these verses should be rendered as "happy," as he himself translates it in *The Explanatory Notes upon the New Testament*.[25] In his third discourse on the Sermon on the Mount, Wesley states that Matthew 5:9 shifts attention from the religion of the heart to the way inward holiness actively expresses itself.[26] He interprets

23. John Wesley, *Works*, 4:67.
24. Ibid., 3:189–91.
25. Ibid., 1:475.
26. Ibid., 1:517.

Jesus's reference to "peacemakers" to encompass all that a Christian ought to do, not only calming strife and contention, but also doing good to everyone. The peacemaker "does good, not of one particular kind, but good in general," including providing food and clothing to those in need of it, taking in the stranger, and visiting the sick and imprisoned.[27] In his *Explanatory Notes*, Wesley explains that the Beatitudes, which speak of holiness of heart and life together, convey Jesus's teaching on "the complete art of happiness," providing his hearers (and readers) with the method for acquiring the goal that every person instinctively pursues.[28] Translating the Greek as "happy," then, is not simply a matter of linguistic concern, but more importantly makes clear the purpose of Jesus's words for the goal of Christian life.

Because of the necessity of "doing" for a life of faith, Wesley talks about Christianity as a "social religion."[29] By this phrase he means that many of the essential aspects of true religion cannot be practiced alone. As has already been made clear, wishing well for one's neighbor must be translated into doing well for one's neighbor. So holiness of life certainly depends on interaction with others. What may be less obvious, but which was also important for Wesley, was the insight that holiness of heart also requires interaction. He shows how many dispositions of the heart need to be exercised in community in order to be developed.[30] For instance, one becomes gentle by treating others gently instead of harshly. Removing oneself from the irritations of interactions with other people removes the opportunities to learn patience and forbearance. The happiness that comes with holiness, then, is something that cannot be gained by oneself but is essentially gained in community. Methodism itself became a community in which holiness of heart and life could be put into practice, and therefore where happiness could be gained.

HAPPINESS AND THE METHODIST MOVEMENT

If Wesley understood the Bible to convey a method for gaining true happiness, he also organized his movement in order to follow this method. Wesley organized the Methodist movement to constitute a society

27. Ibid., 1:518–19.

28. John Wesley, *Explanatory Notes upon the New Testament*, 28; Matt 5, note 2.

29. John Wesley, *Works*, 1:533.

30. Ibid., 1:534–35.

within the Church of England, in order to foster greater commitment to Christian discipleship.[31] This organization over time came to include interlocking groups that consisted of local societies, classes, and bands. Methodists were expected to continue to attend their parish churches, where they received communion, but they were also expected to attend regular meetings of Methodists, where they received instruction, correction, and encouragement in gaining "scriptural holiness."[32]

In 1743, Wesley published *The Nature, Design, and General Rules of the United Societies,* in which he outlined the basic structure and requirements of Methodism. In this document, he says that the only requirement for persons who sought admission to a Methodist society was "a desire to flee from the wrath to come, to be saved from their sins." To continue in the society, though, they should evidence their desire for salvation through (1) "doing no harm," that is, avoiding behaviors that would dishonor or lead away from God or hurt another person; (2) "doing good," such as helping others in body and soul; and (3) "attending upon all the ordinances of God," such as public worship and private prayer and study.[33] The expectations, then, for continuing as a Methodist were that one would engage in those practices that cultivated holiness and avoid those practices that countered it. Subdivision of local societies into class meetings provided a way of overseeing how members continued to grow in scriptural holiness.

Methodist membership in a society did not require persons to leave their usual circumstances and separate themselves from the world. David Lowes Watson argues that the class meeting offered members a "pattern of spiritual nurture" that could be followed even in their daily lives.[34] The class meeting served as a place of accountability, but because the class leader was charged "to inquire how their souls prosper," members' responses could range over a number of concerns and were not specifically focused on confession of sin (as band meetings were).[35] Class meetings

31. For a description of how "society" is distinct from "church" or "sect," see Davies, "Introduction."

32. Ibid., 9:24.

33. John Wesley, *Works,* 9:69–75.

34. Watson, *Early Methodist Class Meeting,* 90.

35. The leaders' tasks are listed in *The Nature, Design, and General Rules of the United Societies,* in John Wesley, *Works,* 9:70. Watson notes differences between classes and bands in *Early Methodist Class Meeting,* 93–123.

general reeles

are sometimes called "catechetical" because as members shared the state of their souls and received comments from the leader, they were learning what to expect in their spiritual growth.[36] Watson uses theories of group interaction to explore what was happening in the class meetings, and he notes that the human interaction there would no doubt have included emotional expression and feedback. The high level of cohesion in the groups would have impelled members to resolve any cognitive dissonance that might emerge in their accounts to one another, so they were shaping each other's expectations and values.[37]

The social identity that Methodists gained through class meetings would have been essential to shaping their understanding of happiness. Through their sharing with one another of their struggles and successes, they were gaining a cognitive orientation to life that helped them know what was worthy of being desired. They also found ready encouragement for their pursuit of those things that truly mattered. In addition, they had a place of accountability if they began to stray from the way of salvation. The organization of the movement, then, actually helped members fit their lives into the understanding that would bring wholeness and life. As they learned to value those things God wanted them to value, they were also fulfilled by them. In the eighteenth century, John Murlin wrote, "I now met with my class constantly, to whom I sometimes gave a word of exhortation. And I never found myself more happy than when I was among the children of God."[38]

Methodists also learned about the connection between holiness and happiness through Charles Wesley's hymns.

> Happy the souls to Jesus join'd,
> And sav'd by grace alone,
> Walking in all thy ways we find
> Our heaven on earth begun.
>
> The church triumphant in thy love
> Their mighty joys we know,
> They sing the Lamb in hymns above,
> And we in hymns below.

---

36. Ibid., 119.

37. Ibid., 129–33.

38. Murlin, "The Life of John Murlin," 417–18.

> Thee in thy glorious realm they praise,
> And bow before thy throne,
> We in the kingdom of thy grace,
> The kingdoms are but one.

> The holy to the holiest leads,
> From hence our spirits rise,
> And he that in thy statutes treads
> Shall meet thee in the skies.[39]

Charles Wesley understands the happiness that Christians experience now to mirror and anticipate the happiness to come, and the way to this happiness is walking in God's ways as they are known to us in God's statutes. Even the children of Methodists learned this connection between holiness and happiness through hymns written especially for them. For instance, a hymn about "the redemption of man" begins:

> Happy the man, who Jesus knows,
> By holy faith to Jesus join'd!
> His pure believing heart o'erflows
> With love to God, and all mankind.

The second verse then describes the happy person's holiness of heart and life

> Redeem'd from all iniquity,
> From every evil work and word,
> From every sinful temper free,
> He lives devoted to his Lord.[40]

Another hymn shows happiness as the design for humanity.

> Bid me in thine image rise
> A saint, a creature new,
> True, and merciful, and wise,
> And pure, and happy too:
> This thy primitive design,
> That I should in thee be blest,
> Should within the arms divine
> Forever ever rest.[41]

---

39. Charles Wesley, "Happy the Souls to Jesus join'd," verses 1–4.
40. Charles Wesley, "Happy the Man who Jesus knows," verses 1–2.
41. Charles Wesley, "Maker, Saviour of Mankind," verse 2.

Beginning early and reinforced through time by theology and practice, the link between holiness and happiness was quite strong for early Methodists.

Given the connection between holiness and happiness in Wesley's theology and Methodist practice, it is not surprising that Methodists used the language of happiness in their accounts of their spiritual lives. Many could speak of happiness when they related stories of hearing preaching, conversion, entire sanctification, and even death.[42] George Story recounts that his resistance to turning to God was first breached when a Methodist woman asked him if he was happy.[43] In his desire for happiness, he devoted himself to God as he had not been able to do before. Ann Gilbert wrote, "I have always found that the more diligent I was in using the means of Grace . . . the more happiness I have enjoyed in my soul."[44] Toward the end of her life, Grace Bennet wrote,

> My happiest days were when I rose at 4 o'clock for prayer, and preaching at five. And I would say it to the praise and glory of God, I find it no cross at this day (being in my 84th year) to rise early to wait upon God with his people no more than when I was *thirty*.[45]

Seeking scriptural holiness was not a dry and dull endeavor, nor was it considered a burden. Becoming fit for relationship with God allowed Methodists to enjoy the fulfillment that relationship with God brings.

Both Wesley's theology and organization aimed at happiness through holiness. The theology and practices that formed the heart taught Methodists what to desire and how to desire it. They desired above all else to make their lives fit for relationship with God, and their practices helped them satisfy that desire. They were happy, then, in the usual sense of that word in their time as satisfied desire. The way they brought holiness and happiness together, though, made happiness more than simply an internal experience of satisfied desire. Happiness depended on love, and love had to be acted out. Happiness as living appropriately

---

42. See for instance Jackson, *Lives of Early Methodist Preachers*, and Chilcote, *Her Own Story*.

43. Jackson, *Lives of Early Methodist Preachers*, 5:228.

44. Chilcote, *Her Own Story*, 51.

45. Ibid., 75–76.

was displayed through holy action. Because happiness was so connected to holiness, a happy life could also be considered an admirable and commendable life. Through their formation in Methodist theology, individuals learned what was truly worth desiring above all else and how properly to enjoy the gifts of God in the created order. Through the accountability structure they received external correction or confirmation that their lives fit God's intent for their natures. External confirmation would undoubtedly increase the internal satisfaction that individuals gained, so this path led to a "good life" in both senses—praiseworthy and rewarding.[46]

Although it seems clear that happiness was a central idea and experience of early Methodism, this happiness cannot simply be described as feeling good. Being happy in God did not mean giddiness, nor did it preclude other, less elevated feelings. Using the word *happiness* to express the fulfillment that comes with fitting one's life to God's raised—and raises—questions about the relation of this happiness to other emotional possibilities for human beings. The next chapter will focus on the some of those questions.

---

46. A holy life was seen as praiseworthy within the society, where values were shared, but as we shall see in the next chapter, a holy life could also lead to reproach by those outside the society who did not share these values.

6

John Wesley: Happiness and Feeling Good

WE SAW IN CHAPTER 3 that there were some tendencies in English religion toward intense introspection to test one's "inner life" for authenticity. Wesley's theology, with its stress on holiness of heart (as well as assurance of salvation), could also tend in this direction. Did connecting happiness with holiness mean that a truly holy person would feel good all the time? Conversely, would not feeling good suggest that something was wrong with one's holiness?[1] The openness with which Methodists shared the state of their souls gave Wesley a realistic understanding about what a Christian could expect with regard to feeling good and helped him see possibilities for understanding happiness as something more than what people refer to as a good mood. Although he did not develop these ideas thoroughly, he did make some observations that indicate he recognized complexity of emotions in spiritual life that could account for sadness as well as happiness. To display the complexity he saw, this chapter will first explore some of his reservations about thinking of true happiness as simply feeling good, then it will examine the notion of "heaviness" in Wesley's work.

---

1. I am using "feeling good" here to mean a consciously subjective condition that is evaluated as positive and pleasurable.

HAPPINESS AND LEVITY

In chapter 4, we saw how Wesley distinguished happiness from levity. For him, being merry was not the same as being happy. Seeking happiness in the pleasures of the world can produce levity—a light-heartedness that lasts for a time. It cannot, though, lead to true Christian happiness—a steady security and fulfillment in God received first by grace and then developed by constant attention to fitting one's life to God's design for human nature. We have seen that Wesley did not rule out taking pleasure in things, but he saw a critical difference between taking pleasure in things simply to gain the good feeling that they bring and taking pleasure in them as God's good gifts—received gratefully and enjoyed responsibly.

The matter of how to take pleasure in created things is connected to the problem of idolatry and desire that has already been explored in previous chapters. To this problem of desire, Wesley added the problem of distraction. Wesley often associates levity with amusements and diversions, things that distract one from living a godly life. A person does not get "time off" from being a Christian. Recognizing that one's entire life belongs to God means that every activity should honor God. This recognition does not mean that one's life should be completely without diversion, but it does mean making good choices about the kind of diversion in which one engages.

Wesley's sermon "The More Excellent Way" in part contains advice about diversions appropriate for a Christian. He says, "But we cannot always be intent upon business; both our bodies and minds require some relaxation. We need intervals of diversion from business."[2] He goes on to list different kinds of diversions, many of which he sees as frankly disreputable, and others that have a tendency to profaneness. Of the latter group, he allows that there may be those who can engage in some of them with a clear conscience, but he also says he cannot do so. Even after acknowledging that there may be "innocent diversions," Wesley calls readers to a "more excellent way" even for amusement. Time for reading may be used to improve the mind, time for conversation may be spent relieving the isolation of the poor and the sick by visiting with them, and praying to God may be the best refreshment of all.[3] Wesley's point seems to be that Christians should avoid amusements that would be hurtful to their souls by distracting them from their proper relationship with God,

2. John Wesley, *Works*, 3:272.

3. Ibid., 3:272–74.

and they should try to increase their use of time in engaging in activities that make their lives more fit for relationship with God. Christians may do things that are fun, but fun is not the measure of their happiness.

One sign of levity was laughter, and Wesley did not express very positive ideas about laughter.[4] His attitude toward laughter has to be understood in the context of the more general discomfort with laughter in his time and place. English understanding of laughter had been influenced by Thomas Hobbes, who had written that laughter had its basis in a feeling of superiority, in other words, enjoying and therefore laughing at another person's failures, weaknesses, or mistakes. The fourth Earl of Chesterfield saw laughing as an activity of the lower classes, not worthy of a gentleman (smiling was acceptable, but not laughing).[5] Although there were others who saw laughter more positively (such as Francis Hutcheson), it was common to think of laughter as impolite. Several of Wesley's explicit references to laughter associate it with scorn or scoffing that comes from a feeling of superiority. Scornful laughter was directed frequently toward Methodists, and Wesley was aware that this unkind laughter was not only hurtful, but could also dissuade those laughed at from following the way of salvation.[6] Scorn was such a common reaction to Wesley and Methodists that one time the lack of laughter at his preaching made him wonder whether he had failed to preach the Gospel as he should.[7] The general discomfort with laughter in his era for Wesley was magnified by particular laughing at Methodism.

Despite Lord Chesterfield's view that laughing belonged to the lower classes, Wesley's journal entries suggest that the gentry were more prone to laughing and talking during worship services than the common folk. People of higher station may have been less attentive than people of lower station because they thought of themselves in less need,

4. Clapper calls attention to Wesley's note to Romans 12:15, in which he says that laughter does not suit a Christian well. Clapper acknowledges this view may be "extreme," but at least helps distinguish genuine Christian happiness from levity. *John Wesley on Religious Affections*, 88–89.

5. For a discussion of laughter in eighteenth-century England, see chapter 1 of Bilger, *Laughing Feminism*, 15–36, and especially nn. 1 and 2. See also Gatrell, *City of Laughter*, 159–77. Gatrell's book also shows that what provoked laughter was often quite crude, and so one can see how Wesley would not think it fitting for Methodists to join in.

6. John Wesley mentions an opponent Dr. Free, who could "laugh and scold and witticize and call names" (*Works*, 21:162). He also warns that being laughed at could tempt Methodists to abandon appropriate behavior (ibid., 3:256).

7. See journal entry, John Wesley, *Works*, 20:377.

or perhaps because they thought of themselves as "above" the rules of conduct in this setting. Occasionally, Wesley notes when the gentry were as attentive to his preaching as the others, presumably because such behavior was not expected.[8] Laughter during preaching indicated that people were distracted from learning how to gain the one thing they needed the most, namely, the restoration of the image of God. Naturally, this distraction would be of great concern to Wesley. Furthermore, if the gentry were normally expected to refrain from laughing, then their behavior in worship, where attention was expected, was an especially poor breach of etiquette.

Clearly, Wesley could think of laughter as impolite, but he could also think of it in even harsher terms. He could see fits of uncontrollable laughter as the work of Satan. A few instances of "involuntary laughter" are recorded in his journals, including a time when he himself was taken over by laughter.[9] The breach of politeness together with the inability to control oneself must have made such an occasion truly shocking and disturbing. Uncontrollable fits were not unknown in the religious life of England, but they were associated with enthusiasm, about which more will be said below. It is not surprising that Wesley would regard fits of laughter negatively.

These reservations about laughter do not necessarily mean that Wesley was opposed to having good humor. Some of his contemporaries or near contemporaries remarked on his cheerfulness and affability— and even his wit—although it should be noted his critics sometimes held a quite different estimation of his personality as dour.[10] Furthermore, Wesley's view of laughter was not entirely negative. He believed Christians could laugh in the face of suffering and destruction, instead of being broken by it, because they have the consolation of the Holy

---

8. See journal entries, ibid., 20:229 and 20:273.

9. For his own experience, see journal entry, ibid., 19:148–49. For an account of Elizabeth Booth, see journal entry, ibid., 20:461–63.

10. Alexander Knox, who knew Wesley personally, wrote, "His countenance, as well as conversation, expressed an habitual gayety of heart," in "Remarks on the Life and Character of John Wesley," 344. Some anecdotes are recorded in Hurst, *John Wesley the Methodist*, 304–7. More anecdotes, along with a description of Wesley by his niece, are in Telford, *Life of John Wesley*, 354–65. In his reply to a critic about the enthusiasm of Methodists, Wesley writes that he is charged as "not willing to indulge himself in the least levity of behaviour, or in laughter." Wesley does not deny this charge, but only denies that he adopts seriousness for effect. See John Wesley, *Works*, 11:363.

Spirit.[11] He records that once when he had a fever he laughed when he felt the joy of God's comfort in his time of illness.[12] Wesley's remarks about laughter are few, they are shaped by cultural expectations and particular experiences, and they do not offer anything like a general theory of the appropriateness of laughter for Christian life. Christians living in a different time may judge the value of laughter more positively, even acknowledging its benefit to health. Still, Wesley's remarks about laughter and levity do have relevance for reflection on happiness. Genuine Christian happiness cannot be built on ridicule of others, nor on any sense of feeling superior to someone else. It is not gained when we allow light-heartedness to distract us from paying attention to God. Neither feeling good at someone else's expense nor the good feeling that comes from frivolous activity constitutes the happiness that Wesley paired with holiness. The happiness that God wants for us is not a superficial and temporary feeling but a deep and lasting fulfillment.

HAPPINESS AND ENTHUSIASM

Perhaps one contributing factor to the way Wesley regarded laughter is that Methodists were often the targets of satire on account of their "enthusiasm," and the laughing ridicule they received must surely have been hard for him to bear. The most basic meaning of "enthusiasm" was "immediate inspiration," but by the seventeenth century in England it had come to be used as a "false claim to inspiration" because it had been associated with groups that claimed inspiration (such as Quakers and Ranters) that were outside the established order.[13] By the eighteenth century, it could be extended to "extreme conduct of many kinds," namely, whatever threatened the moderation and order prized by society.[14] Frenzy, false doctrine, and rigorous behavior could all receive the charge of enthusiasm, and Methodists were satirized in all these areas.[15]

The early Methodist movement in England did include some frenzied physical expressions reminiscent of enthusiastic sects of the previous century, but although Methodist meetings remained emotional,

11. John Wesley, *Works*, 1:425.

12. See journal entry, ibid., 19:238.

13. Lee, *Historical Backgrounds*, 58.

14. Ibid., 114. For instance, the charge mentioned in n. 10 that Wesley never laughed shows concern about extreme seriousness rather than frenzy.

15. See Lyles, *Methodism Mocked*.

the physical effects that marked the beginning of the movement do not seem to have continued for very many years.[16] Wesley's supervision of the movement allowed expression of emotion but kept it from becoming dangerously unrestrained.[17] In his writings, he often uses the words "calm" and "peace," rather than ecstatic language, to describe the happiness that real Christians experience. Although there was certainly a good feeling that accompanied assurance of God's love, that feeling was more comforting than it was wild and exciting. Furthermore, ecstatic enthusiasm could never be what Wesley meant by happiness because he had in mind not a fleeting feeling of euphoria, but a way of life.

Although powerful feelings were associated with Methodism, Wesley was aware that for many people then (just as for many people now) the initial feeling of happiness that comes from experiencing God's love can fade over time. Wesley writes that even though Christian happiness begins when "it pleases the Father to reveal his Son in our heart," some went on to ask, "whether it is the design of God that the happiness which is at first enjoyed by all that know and love him should continue any longer than, as it were, the day of their espousals." To this question, Wesley replies, "In very many, we must allow, it does not; but in a few months, perhaps weeks, or even days, the joy and peace either vanish at once, or gradually decay. Now if God is willing that their happiness should continue, how is this to be accounted for?"[18] Wesley accounts for this fading of happiness after the initial powerful experience by citing Jude 21: "Keep yourselves in the love of God." This imperative "implies that something is to be done on our part in order to its continuance."[19]

If one's initial happiness fades, it is because one has not actively sought to grow in grace. God provides many means of grace for our growth, but we must make use of them in order to benefit from them. By using the means of grace, we will continue to grow in love, and as our love increases so will our happiness. For Wesley, then, happiness is not simply the good feeling that is gained from the initial knowledge of God's love for us. However important that may be, it must continue to be cultivated by a disciplined Christian life. Happiness is maintained

16. Lyles says that they had stopped by the early 1740s (*Methodism Mocked*, 102). Public impressions of frenzied meetings continued, though, for many years after that.

17. Lee, *Historical Backgrounds*, 144–46.

18. John Wesley, *Works*, 3:283.

19. Ibid.

through fostering holiness. The happiness that lasts is not simply a brief feeling or even a good mood, but is the rich fulfillment of knowing one is steadily making use of God's grace to grow in love.

HAPPINESS AND HEAVINESS

The happiness that comes from "fitting" into God's design by fulfilling the end of one's nature is purposeful, and so it is quite different from happiness that depends simply on "what happens," that is, on the good feelings that arise from living in favorable circumstances. In fact, purposeful happiness may exist even in circumstances that are normally understood to be unfavorable. Because Wesley has not simply equated happiness with feeling good, he has intellectual space to explore the relation of less elevated feelings to Christian happiness under the notion of "heaviness."

By 1760, Wesley had become aware enough of the anxiety many felt about needing to be assured of their salvation that he wrote a pair of sermons to address this concern.[20] In these sermons, he distinguishes "darkness" from "heaviness." "The Wilderness State" describes the state of darkness, in which faith, love, joy, peace, and therefore power over sin have been lost. In this state, righteousness is also lost, and so a person in darkness is no longer traveling on the way of salvation.[21] As he explains in "Heaviness through Manifold Temptations," the state of heaviness is quite different from the state of darkness. Although persons in a state of heaviness experience trials, they have not lost their faith, peace, hope, love, or holiness.[22] They remain, then, on the way of salvation even through very difficult life situations.

Wesley describes heaviness as sorrow or grief, which everyone knows at least as a passion (that is, on account of a particular object and lasting only a period of time), but it is for some even more—a "settled temper" that "having taken fast hold of the heart is not presently shaken off, but continues for some time." Described as a settled temper, heaviness sounds like what we now call depression. Wesley describes this temper as "so deep as to overshadow the whole soul, to give a colour, as it were, to all the affections, such as will appear in the whole behaviour. It

20. Ibid., 2:202.
21. Ibid., 2:205–21.
22. Ibid., 2:222–35.

may likewise have an influence over the body."[23] What distinguishes this settled temper from darkness is that even with this "inward affliction" believers can rejoice.[24] That is, they may be grateful to God, they may enjoy relationship with God, and they may trust that whatever else may be uncertain in their lives, God's love is sure.

The causes of heaviness are many, including acute or chronic bodily disorders, pain of any sort, calamity, poverty, and the waywardness or death of loved ones. All of these conditions may cause grief and sorrow, but in Wesley's thinking God permits these circumstances because they may also lead to greater faith, hope, love, and holiness. They serve as trials in the sense of tests that strengthen us. Just as fire purifies gold from its dross, hardship purifies faith from trust in any created thing so that we depend on nothing other than God. Wesley reasons that with greater faith comes greater hope for immortality, so we have cause for rejoicing even in sorrow. We also become even more grateful to God for being the sure ground of our trust, which increases our love. As love for God increases, so also does love for others.

Heaviness, then, when recognized and used by a believer as an opportunity for growth, can lead to "unspeakable gain" that is cause for rejoicing. A person in heaviness has not lost the peace of God, having "a soul calm and serene in the midst of storms, sorrowful, yet always rejoicing,"[25] so happiness exists even in heaviness, not as a simple good feeling, but as fulfillment in a stronger relationship with God and in one's greater conformity to the mind of Christ, who also suffered. The corollary to saying there is no "time off" from being a Christian is that if our lives belong to God, no event, no matter how difficult, falls outside God's concern and the relevance of Christian faith.

Grief and sorrow are felt especially keenly at a time of death, but for Wesley, mourning for someone's death is lessened when one knows the loved one is happy with God fully and finally in the next life. When he was young (in January 1726/27), Wesley preached at the funeral of Robin Griffiths, a friend from Oxford, and his sermon cautioned the gathered family and friends against "profusely sorrowing" over the death of this young man. He directed their thinking to the happiness that Griffiths now enjoyed with God and tried to comfort them with the

23. Ibid., 2:224–25.
24. Ibid.
25. Ibid., 2:233.

thought that they would join him and experience the same happiness after not so long a time. Although some "parting pangs" would surely be felt, they should not be dwelt on and should be countered with reminders that their separation will not be long.[26] John Wesley's idea of what would comfort family and friends in this sermon may not meet current standards of pastoral care, but in his time, it was common to see death not only as a release from the cares of this world, but also—for faithful pilgrims—as a good end to their journey.

Like John, Charles Wesley also stressed happiness over mourning in the face of death. He published a collection of funeral hymns, a few of them written on the occasion of the death of particular individuals, and references to happiness in these hymns are many. The first verses of a hymn for Mrs. A. C. echo the sentiments of John's sermon:

> And is the struggle past,
> And hath she groan'd her last?
> Rise, my soul, and take thy flight,
> Haste, th' ascending triumph share,
> Trace her to the plains of light,
> Grasp her happy spirit there!
>
> I *know* her now possest
> Of everlasting rest!
> Now I *find* her lodg'd above,
> Now her heavenly joy I *feel*,
> Extasy of joy and love,
> Glorious and unspeakable.
>
> I triumph in her bliss;
> The proof, the token this!
> This my dying friend's bequest,
> This the answer of her prayer,
> Speaks her entred into rest,
> Tells me I shall meet her there.[27]

No sorrow is expressed in these verses (or in the entire hymn). Because the struggle is over for the one who has died, she may feel joy in its fullest. And because those who remain know she is happy, they may share in her happiness. The Wesleys could speak of so much happiness at the time of a loved one's death because they saw the death of a faithful Christian as

26. Ibid., 4:242.
27. Charles Wesley, "And Is the Struggle Past?" verses 1–3.

a release from the trials of this life and the culmination of their journey toward God. As Charles says in another funeral hymn:

> Rejoice for a brother decease'd,
> (Our loss is his infinite gain)
> A soul out of prison releas'd,
> And freed from its bodily chain:
> With songs let us follow his flight,
> And mount with his spirit above,
> Escap'd to the mansions of light,
> And lodg'd in the Eden of love.[28]

Release from the difficulties of this life brings a freedom and opportunity to enjoy love to the utmost, and it is this freedom that Charles highlights and celebrates.

Over time, perhaps because of pastoral sensitivity or personal experience (as by this time several close family members had died), Wesley became more willing to acknowledge sorrow at the time of a loved one's death. By the time John Wesley wrote "Heaviness through Manifold Temptations" (1760), he had become more willing to admit the sadness even faithful Christians could feel. After naming ways that the circumstances of a loved one's death may add to its distress, he says, "In all these cases we not only may, but ought to be affected: it is the design of God that we should. He would not have us stocks and stones. He would therefore have our affections regulated, not extinguished. . . . There may be sorrow without sin."[29] So over time, Wesley came to acknowledge that the death of a loved one could bring great heaviness. Wesley could include this sorrow and grief under the term "heaviness," though, because it did not exclude happiness in God. In fact, it was precisely because of one's relationship with God that one could bear the heaviness of a loved one's death and not fall into the utter despair that Wesley called darkness.

Another sign that Wesley could adjust his thinking about happiness to extreme circumstances appears in the very sermon in which he makes the claim "that every Christian is happy and that he who is not happy is not a Christian." This claim is intended to express how central happiness is to true religion, but in the very next paragraph, Wesley names exceptions to that claim: those who are "under violent temptation" or "under deep nervous disorders, which are indeed a species of insanity" (what

---

28. Charles Wesley, "Rejoice for a brother deceas'd," verse 1.
29. John Wesley, *Works*, 3:228.

we today would call mental illness) may be overwhelmed and have their happiness suspended.[30] It seems to me that by allowing these exceptions, Wesley is both trying to hold on to an insight about Christian faith that he takes to be key for illuminating its purpose and essence, but he is also trying to acknowledge the very real hardships that some people face that keep them from experiencing the fullness of life that God intends. If he did not succeed in navigating the right way between these two insights, he has at least seen the problem and made it clear for those who follow. It is the task of those who have better resources for understanding circumstances such as mental illness to think about how to talk about God's presence through this kind of suffering.

Not only do the circumstances of life bring sorrow and grief, but Wesley recognized that religion itself implies a certain suffering. Wesley asks whether for the Christian, this suffering "impairs or heightens happiness." In answering the question, he reiterates the possibility of rejoicing in one's own accidental circumstances of "loss, poverty, or pain," but he also recognizes that "love of neighbour will give rise to sympathizing sorrow" for another in need.[31] A Christian who truly loves neighbors cannot help but feel pain when those neighbors feel pain. It is in this case the very nature of Christian faith itself that can lead to sorrow. The more one loves as a Christian should, the more one opens oneself to hurting on another's behalf. Love of neighbor, though, will not only bring sympathizing sorrow; it will also propel a Christian to take action to relieve the suffering of others. Through this action, the fruits of true religion actually contribute to happiness—both for the ones whose suffering is relieved and for the ones who acted, as they rejoice in having been the instruments of God to aid another. To return to Wesley's question, then, this suffering neither impairs happiness, nor simply coexists with it, but actually heightens it.

In other sermons, Wesley mentions two other ways religion implies suffering or sorrow. First, Christians may not only be grieved by circumstances, but also by their sin. Deep knowledge of oneself combined with increased knowledge of the majesty of God can display the difference between oneself and God so thoroughly that one feels the heaviness of sin all the more in light of God's goodness. Wesley notes that some have confused this heaviness with darkness, but he points out that conviction

30. Ibid., 3:100.
31. Ibid., 3:190–92.

of sin is itself a step on the way of salvation.[32] God uses this sorrow to draw us closer, so grief over sin is actually a step on the way to happiness. Wesley uses this idea about heaviness in sin to explain the verse "Blessed are they that mourn; for they shall be comforted." He takes this beatitude to refer to the mourning of believers over the temptation and sin that remains in them even after they are justified. This realization without doubt produces a time of heaviness, but those who do not turn from the way of salvation will be comforted, and that comfort turns sadness into joy.[33]

Charles Wesley expresses both the sorrow and the joy of those who mourn in this way:

> Why then do thy fears return?
> Yet again why dost thou mourn?
> Whence the clouds that round thee roll?
> Whence the doubts that tear thy soul?
> Why are all thy comforts fled?
> "Sin revives, and I am dead."
> Dead alas! Thou art within,
> Still remains the inbred sin,
> Dead within thou surely art,
> Still unclean remains thy heart;
> Pride and self are still behind,
> Still the earthly carnal mind,
> The untam'd rebellious will,
> Foe to good, inslav'd to ill;
> Still the nature unrenew'd,
> Alien from the life of God.

The realization that the struggle with sin continues provokes mourning. Deadness and enslavement to sin drive out all comfort.

> Mourn awhile for God thy rest,
> God will soon pronounce thee blest,
> Soon the Comforter will come,
> Fix in thee his constant home,
> With thy heart his witness bear
> Strong, and permanent, and clear:
> All thy griefs shall then be gone,
> Doubt, and fear no more be known,
> Holy love thy heart possess,

32. Ibid., 2:230–31.
33. Ibid., 1:483–86.

> Silent joy, and steadfast peace,
> Peace that never can decay,
> Joy that none can take away.

The hymn offers encouragement that God will bless the mourner with the lasting witness of the Holy Spirit, which will eliminate the doubt and fear that remain and replace them with joy and peace.

> Happy soul, as silver tried,
> Silver seven times purified,
> Love hath broke the rock of stone,
> All thy hardness melted down,
> Wrath, and pride, and hatred cease,
> All thy heart is gentleness.
> Let the waves around thee rise,
> Let the tempest threat the skies,
> Calm thou ever art within,
> All unruffled, all serene:
> Thy sure anchor cannot fail,
> Enter'd now within the veil;
> Glad this earth thou canst resign:
> The new heavens and earth are thine.[34]

Although believers feel the weight of their remaining "inbred sin," this hymn reminds them of their hope for joy to come. Once tried and purified, the "happy soul" may expect to be "calm" "serene," and "glad."

Second, living in holiness opens a person to reproach. One would think that persons would be honored for living an intentionally Christian life, but Wesley points out that they are in fact persecuted. Of course, Jesus's disciples cannot expect to escape what he himself suffered, and indeed they should understand persecution as "the very badge of [their] discipleship."[35] Because those who are persecuted for righteousness' sake are blessed, those who suffer in this way may still rejoice because they come closer to entering the kingdom of God.

Christians cannot expect to avoid sorrow, and so some heaviness will accompany their pursuit of happiness. Sometimes that sorrow comes simply because of circumstances that all humans face. At other times it comes precisely when Christians seek happiness through holiness. It is the ability to interpret the events that cause sorrow within their understanding of growth in relationship to God that prevents faithful Christians from

34. Charles Wesley, "Who believes the tidings?" verses 5–7.
35. John Wesley, *Works*, 1:525.

being overcome and eventually strengthens that relationship. Rejoicing in sorrow, then, does not mean denying sadness at the time it is felt. Instead, it is anticipation that events that cause sadness may be used by God so that they may ultimately contribute to fulfillment. The confidence that one may continue to rely on God through heaviness provides comfort, and that very reliance fits one's life to God's design for human nature, so it contributes to happiness in the sense that Wesley intends.

Locke had taught his age to categorize life in terms of pleasure and pain, happiness and misery. Wesley adopted this categorization to the extent that his theology aimed to help Christians seek happiness and escape misery, but for him there was no simple equation between happiness and pleasure, or between misery and pain. Although Christian happiness is a positive experience, it cannot be reduced simply to good feelings for two reasons: first, feelings may be elevated and pleasurable even when they do not fit with God's design for humanity; and second, Christian happiness is compatible with sorrow. These two qualifications make sense in light of the cognitive aspect of Christian happiness. Christians are happy *about* something, namely, about attaining the end of their nature so they are fit for relationship with God. So on the one hand, ridicule is not an adequate means of bringing the fulfillment that true happiness is about because it is not an expression of love for neighbor. Similarly, amusements may not advance a person toward this fulfillment. On the other hand, when the events that bring pain and sorrow inevitably come, they need not lead directly to misery. Understanding what it means to regain the image of God makes it possible to interpret those events so that heaviness does not become darkness. To the extent that happiness is a feeling it is a feeling of fulfillment, it is a conscious sensation of God's love that enables one to become more loving. As one learns to love as God loves, one then gains satisfaction according to God's design for human nature. This satisfaction is not simply a transient positive sensation but an ongoing sense of gratitude and benevolence that for Wesley constitutes true religion and true happiness.

With this understanding of Christian happiness in mind, I turn now to explore some of the current thinking about happiness that is being disseminated in the wider culture. It is this understanding of happiness that forms the context in which Christians today offer their vision of what happiness is.

7

A Theology of Happiness and the New Study of Happiness

THE FIELD OF PSYCHOLOGY has long paid attention to problems that reduce happiness for humans, but recently attention is shifting from treating negative patient conditions to promoting human flourishing. While this shift is a fairly recent development (about two decades old), it is gaining momentum. Attention to disabling pathologies, while still important, is being joined with attention to those things that make people feel satisfied with their lives. Research is rapidly expanding our understanding of happiness. Not only is this research seeking to name what constitutes happiness, it also is resulting in suggestions for how to promote happiness. This research has contributed to a widespread popular interest in the topic. Almost daily, some article or blog post will appear on the Internet about how to become happier.[1] The topic of happiness has appeared frequently of late in magazines, newspapers, and books.

As in the eighteenth century, the language of happiness is everywhere. Just as John Wesley critically engaged with the "culture of

---

1. For instance, Gretchen Rubin has been trying out tips for happiness in her own life for a book—*The Happiness Project: Or, Why I Spent a Year Trying to Sing in the Morning, Clean My Closets, Fight Right, Read Aristotle, and Generally Have More Fun*—and reporting the results on her daily blog http://www.happiness-project.com/happiness_project/ (accessed August 25, 2009).

happiness" in his time, Christians in the twenty-first century have the opportunity to be in conversation with the larger culture about what Christian happiness is. Having provided a view of Christian happiness in the previous chapters, this chapter seeks to encourage and inform this conversation by presenting some major ideas that are contributing to the rapidly growing "culture of happiness" that is developing in our time. To do so, it will focus on a few resources that attempt to make the new research accessible to the general public.

POSITIVE PSYCHOLOGY

In the past, psychology has mostly focused on helping people whose lives had become difficult in some way to regain a normal level of functioning, but in recent decades, that goal has seemed to be set too low. With all the resources for understanding human life at its disposal, many have wondered why psychology should not try to enrich human living instead of simply helping people to operate at some average level that makes life bearable but not particularly enjoyable. This question has given rise to a new focus within the field. The term "positive psychology" was coined by Martin E. P. Seligman in the 1990s to describe the study of "positive emotion, positive character, and positive institutions."[2] As Christopher Peterson puts it in his *Primer in Positive Psychology*, "Positive psychology is the scientific study of what goes right in life, from birth to death and at all the stops in between. It is the newly christened approach within psychology that takes seriously as a subject matter those things that make life most worth living."[3] A growing number of studies have begun to examine when and how people feel levels of satisfaction with their lives that can be described as "happy." As a new field, positive psychology is still developing and will uncover much more through research over the coming years. Psychologists are already, though, beginning to think about what the current research findings mean for how people ought to live their lives.[4] Although insights continue to unfold, a few key ideas provide some orientation to the work that is going on.

In any field, it is important to specify what is being studied. Happiness is not the only positive emotion that makes life worth living, but it is

2. Seligman et al., "Positive Psychology Progress," 410–21.

3. Peterson, *Primer in Positive Psychology*, 4.

4. Two good examples are Myers, *Pursuit of Happiness*, and Haidt, *Happiness Hypothesis*.

one significant area for the field of positive psychology. Peterson suggests that the study of happiness may function as a subfield under positive psychology, in which researchers specify and study particular manifestations of happiness.[5] For instance, he notes that philosophy has offered two distinct routes to happiness through pleasure and virtue. Psychology can study these two routes (as well as others that may be identified) to try to measure the extent to which each route leads to life satisfaction or subjective well-being. In his glossary, Peterson defines *happiness* as "everyday synonym for subjective well-being, life satisfaction, and the like." He further defines "life satisfaction" as "overall cognitive appraisal that one's life is a good one," and "subjective well-being" as "relatively high levels of positive affect, relatively low levels of negative affect, and the overall judgment that one's life is a good one."[6]

Peterson explains some of the complexities that present themselves to a psychological study of happiness. As a social science, research in psychology deals in measurement, but determining what to measure and how to measure it can be tricky. For instance, if one is measuring pleasure, is the best method to ask people to report on their experiences of the moment (experience sampling) or to summarize the "trajectory and pattern of their lives." In the former, one gains immediacy and context, but loses sequence and evaluation. In the latter, one gains the "big picture," but that picture depends on memory that can be unreliable.[7]

Alternatively, using an understanding of happiness as satisfied desire, one could measure the extent to which one has gained what one desires. Whether measuring pleasure or satisfied desire, a researcher depends largely on self-reporting by individuals because only they know what pleases them or what they desire. Because self-defined pleasures and desires may not be adequate by themselves for describing a good life, some have suggested the need for an objective list of things that are good for people, such as material comfort, health, and education. Questions then arise about what belongs on the list, and further, some have observed that self-reporting of satisfaction does not always correlate with having what is on the list. For instance, depression has risen at the same time that access to material goods has increased. Researchers in psychology, then, have mostly opted for self-reports through surveys

5. Peterson, *Primer in Positive Psychology*, 78–80.

6. Ibid., 104.

7. Ibid., 81–82.

or interviews, and Peterson says, "This approach to measuring happiness as a subjective experience has much to recommend it because it resonates with how most of us think about happiness. Happiness is a personal experience and indeed an idiosyncratic one."[8] What makes one person happy does not necessarily make another person happy.

Even if the causes of happiness may vary, one of the insights gained by these types of measurement is that some manifestations of happiness are more lasting than others. It is very common for human beings to focus the search for happiness on satisfying desires in order to feel pleasure, and indeed, a human being feels good when certain activities release the chemical dopamine in the brain. Two things, though, work against this experience as true or lasting happiness. First, it seems that human beings can find more pleasure in making progress toward a goal than in actually reaching the goal itself. Pleasure in the final result when the desire is actually satisfied may not be much better than pleasure one has experienced along the way; and even if one experiences something like euphoria at the end, it will only last as long as the dopamine lasts. Second, human beings have a tendency to adapt to circumstances, so achieving a goal and remaining there quickly loses its ability to make one feel better than before. We need a new goal, but if we set as our new goal simply more of what has previously brought us pleasure (such as gaining more money), we will quickly adapt to that level, too.[9] Pleasure simply does not bring lasting happiness.

So what does? One component of an answer to that question is undertaking activity that involves us in such a way that we are completely absorbed in it. Psychologists describe this experience as "flow," the feeling of being "lost" in a task, of being conscious only of the activity itself so that time seems to fly by. One way to gain this feeling of flow is to undertake a challenging task that suits our strengths so that we are both required to extend our abilities and are successful in doing so. We may also feel flow in other ways, such as through movement and conversation.[10] To capture the significance of flow for happiness, Martin Seligman distinguishes between pleasure, which is based in sense experience and feeling, and gratification, which is based in activities that engage and challenge us.[11]

8. Ibid., 81–84.

9. Haidt, *Happiness Hypothesis*, 81–86.

10. Myers, *Pursuit of Happiness*, 127–41.

11. Haidt, *Happiness Hypothesis*, 96.

Gaining gratification from being absorbed in a challenging task that one is able to accomplish leads to longer lasting mood improvement than does satisfying sensual desires for pleasure. Pleasurable feelings are momentary. We really like them when we have them, but they do not become a part of us. Gratifications, in contrast, come from the exercise of traits that are a part of us, so using them gives us a sense of authentic well-being.[12] In fact, when engaged in gratifying activity we are so absorbed that we do not "feel" at that time.[13] Only after the fact do we say, "I enjoyed that." Using this distinction, it appears that longer lasting gratifications are not simply on a continuum with more temporary pleasures. Both provide "satisfaction," but in different ways.

Relatedness to others is another important component of happiness. We are social creatures through and through, and we need to be attached to and to be intimate with other people. When our relationships are going well, friends, family, spouses all play a role in keeping us healthy. When these relationships go badly, they contribute to stress. In either case, relationships play a central role in how we experience our lives and cope (or do not cope) with the circumstances around us. Happiness is not just an individual accomplishment; the self-disclosure, support, and laughter that we share with others make a real difference in our well-being.[14] These two factors—flow and relatedness—are so important to happiness that the unhappiest people seem to be those who are alone and have nothing that needs to be done.[15]

It is not just what we do or who we have in our lives, though, that makes us happy. Circumstances and genetics also play a role. The situation in which we find ourselves can contribute in positive or negative ways. We do need to have basic needs met, and if they are not, life satisfaction will be low. Once those needs have been met, though, external factors have something of a mixed role in our lives. For instance, the social world in which we live can shape our expectations in such a way that we can either be satisfied with less or crave more.[16] Adversity also can play different roles. For some, catastrophic events can truly traumatize a person to the extent that well-being suffers. For others, having to face

---

12. Seligman, *Authentic Happiness*, 9.

13. Ibid., 111.

14. Myers, *Pursuit of Happiness*, 142–54.

15. Ibid., 137.

16. Ibid., 37–41.

hardship allows one to develop a perspective that may include finding one's strengths, learning what really matters in life, and enhancing relationships.[17] The control that we have over external factors also makes a difference. If we have some ability to make choices in our situation, we feel happier than if we are in situations where we have little or no control over what happens in our lives.[18]

External factors, though, also work with internal factors. Optimism, self-esteem, and having an outgoing personality can all enhance happiness.[19] Traits like these can be cultivated, but they also depend to some extent on genetic predisposition. Twin studies show that there may be a characteristic range of happiness with which each person is born. We can operate at higher or lower levels in that range, depending on the other factors that also count for or against happiness. The complicated interaction of all these various components has led psychologists to suggest a formula for happiness: $H = S + C + V$. In other words, happiness (H) is the combination of the set point (or range) of happiness allowed by one's genes (S), the conditions in which one lives (C), and the voluntary activities in which one engages (V).[20]

In this formula, the element over which one has the most control is clearly V (voluntary activities). Seligman suggests that a good way to find optimal happiness in life is to use one's "signature strengths," because engaging those strengths every day leads to "authentic happiness and abundant gratification."[21] Although many people settle for what he calls "the pleasant life," or having momentary positive emotions, he calls people to "the good life," gained by "using your signature strengths to obtain abundant gratification in the main realms of your life," such as work, love, or parenting. Even beyond the good life, though, is the possibility of "the meaningful life," which puts those signature strengths and virtues in "the service of something larger than you are."[22] Seligman leaves the "something larger" vague, both because Seligman himself does not recommend a particular meaning system for happiness and because meaning systems, like personal strengths and experience of

17. Haidt, *Happiness Hypothesis*, 135–53.

18. Myers, *Pursuit of Happiness*, 113–16.

19. Ibid., 105–26.

20. Haidt, *Happiness Hypothesis*, 90–91.

21. Seligman, *Authentic Happiness*, 13.

22. Ibid., 13–14 and 261–63.

happiness, vary from individual to individual. Seligman does, though, at the end of *Authentic Happiness*, engage in some tentative speculation about meaning.[23]

ALTERNATIVE VOICES

Daniel Gilbert is a psychologist who has not followed the lead of positive psychology to try to find ways of improving happiness in life, but rather he has tried to understand why human beings are so often wrong about what we think will make us happy. His book *Stumbling on Happiness* outlines several ways that the mind works to foresee how we will feel about future choices and situations, and how often that foresight fails us. His book focuses on happiness as a feeling or subjective experience, and he faults philosophers for having muddled this feeling with virtue. They did so, he suggests, because it did not seem worthwhile or noble to use any means to strive for the feeling. They confused, then, the feeling with what they thought ought to be the cause of the feeling, namely, virtuous action. He also faults psychologists for confusing the emotional meaning with matters of judgment. That is, when a person says, "I'm happy about the way things turned out," that statement is not expressing an emotion, but rather a judgment about the merits of the situation. He observes that psychologists have too often taken the expressions "I'm happy about" or "I'm happy that" to be indicators of emotion rather than belief.[24] Gilbert therefore distinguishes emotional happiness (feeling) from moral happiness (performing virtuous actions) from judgmental happiness (approval), and he clearly makes emotional happiness the centerpiece of his book.[25]

Because of his focus, Gilbert has rather controversially questioned the idea that children make parents happy. He observes that parents believe their children should make them happy, so they say they do, although several studies show parents feel less happiness taking care of

23. His speculation is prompted by Robert Wright's *NonZero* thesis that the universe is moving toward complexity with more win-win scenarios. This speculation begins to engage in what seems to me to be highly questionable theology. Seligman, *Authentic Happiness*, 250–60.

24. Because Gilbert does not refer to any specific psychologists in this assessment, it is not possible to know whether he is criticizing what cognitive psychologists have said about the cognitive component of emotion or whether he is ignoring this work.

25. Gilbert, *Stumbling on Happines*, 35–38.

their children than when they are doing other things. These studies are no doubt successful in capturing the momentary feelings that parents have when they do the hard work of child-rearing, but Gilbert may not be correct to conclude from these studies that parents are simply fooling themselves when they say their children make them happy. They may be expressing what Seligman calls gratification rather than merely accepting something they have been told to believe. In other words, they feel satisfaction from the relationships they have built with their children, even when child-rearing tasks require effort and are done with difficulty. Persevering through the difficulty may be part of what the parent finds rewarding. So if Gilbert charges others with a problem of conflation (muddling meanings together), he may be charged with his own muddling, namely, failing to recognize nuances and distinctions that need to be made even on the level of emotion.[26] Momentary subjective feelings do not capture everything that happiness is. Peterson's observations mentioned above about the differences between experience sampling and retrospective evaluation need to be kept in mind.

Gilbert does not directly engage positive psychology as a field, but Eric G. Wilson sees the widespread interest in positive psychology as an expression of a typical state of mind in American culture.[27] Wilson is not himself a psychologist. He describes himself as a "literary humanist searching for a deeper life," whose "basic instinct is toward melancholia."[28] He has written about the relationship between literature and psychology, and he has published his thoughts on happiness and melancholy in the *Chronicle of Higher Education*.[29] For Wilson, the search for religious freedom and the practice of free trade that were present from the beginning in the United States of America were based in a shared optimism about earthly joy that has shaped the culture ever since. The culture seeks "happiness as immediate gratification, happiness as superficial comfort, happiness as static contentment," and by denying sadness it also denies the wisdom about reality that sadness brings.[30] In fact, "happy types" see the world through a "grid" that only acknowledges those things that reinforce their views and must repress counterevidence, including their

26. Ibid., 220–22.
27. Wilson, *Against Happiness*, 5.
28. Ibid., 7 and 39.
29. Wilson, "In Praise of Melancholy."
30. Wilson, *Against Happiness*, 8.

own sadness that shows the world in a different light. Wilson sees the perpetual pursuit of happiness as an effort toward security and control.[31] Where once churches helped people see the world more clearly, now they have become "happiness companies," in which "contrition has turned trite, and contentment has become the given."[32]

Wilson is not against a joy that is earned after facing the genuine troubles of life, instead he is against any oversimplifying that hides complexity and denies the conflicts that have given rise to what he sees as the noblest expressions of the human spirit. Nor does he mean to discount the very real suffering of severe depression, but he thinks that the typical rush to avoid any and all sadness has left us unable to distinguish between disabling depression and the melancholy that can actually motivate people toward change.[33] Like Gilbert, Wilson has restricted the word *happiness* to a single level of meaning, in this case something superficial compared to a mature joy that can handle complexity. As a generalized observation about a culture, Wilson's assessment of popular attention to happiness may be largely correct. Such superficial happiness, though, may not be countered adequately by lauding melancholy. It may also take drawing attention to other kinds of satisfaction that are more lasting and fulfilling.

If Wilson thinks that attention to happiness is a way of avoiding the challenges of life, Vincent Brümmer, in contrast, understands the study of happiness as a way of coping with challenge. He says:

> The rapid cultural changes which are so characteristic of our time, have had a far reaching effect not only on the search for human happiness, well-being and meaningful human existence in our world, but also on the way these concepts are understood and misunderstood in contemporary culture. It has become increasingly unclear what is to count as happiness and well-being and what is to constitute a meaningful existence for human beings in the modern world.[34]

Together with Marcel Sarot, Brümmer edited a volume of papers presented at the Fourth Consultation on Science and Religion sponsored by the Center for Theological Exploration, Inc., at the University of Aarhus

31. Ibid., 24–29.
32. Ibid., 20.
33. Ibid., 7–8.
34. Brümmer, "Preface," vi.

in Denmark, all of which focus in some way on happiness, well-being, and the meaning of life. Brümmer cites the Center's assertion that in the face of the enormous changes taking place in the world, "the most pressing intellectual challenge of our time" is to rethink our ways of understanding that world.[35] Far from being superficial or trivial, then, the study of happiness, well-being, and meaning are profound and crucial topics. In the light of the pressing need for reconceiving value patterns in changing times, the Center encourages theologians to enter into dialogue with the natural and human sciences.

In the introduction to this collection of papers, Sarot notes that inquiry about happiness, well-being, and meaning is evaluative, so it is necessary to understand the standards by which evaluation of life is made. He identifies three levels of standards that should guide analysis:

1. subjective standards: standards that are entirely a matter of personal choice;

2. objective standards: standards that are independent of the human subject;

3. basic standards: standards specifying the basic conditions that have to be fulfilled before a human being can strive after a life that is good in the subjective and objective senses.

Sarot argues that when talking about happiness, it is the subjective standards that pertain, although he also distinguishes between two different meanings of the subjective statement "I am happy." In making this assertion, one might mean "I feel happy," that is, one is currently experiencing an emotional state of contentment. Or one might not intend to express feeling happy but *being* happy, that is, affirming that one's life includes those things that one believes to bring contentment (for instance, "I am happy because I have a good job, no serious disease, and some leisure time for things I enjoy"). In either case the statement is personal, and one individual cannot choose for another individual the standards either for feeling happy or being happy.[36]

It is possible, though, that a person may be mistaken about whether her or his life actually conforms to her or his own standards. Take, for instance, a woman who feels happy in her marriage, and who claims that her marriage is a happy one, but who is unaware that her husband

35. Ibid.

36. Sarot, "Introduction," 3–4.

is unfaithful. Furthermore, people have such an ability to adapt to their conditions that they may feel a certain contentment even in situations that are not good for them. These possibilities open the way for introducing objective standards to the evaluation of human life—not to determine whether or not a person truly feels content, but because other considerations besides contentment have to be taken into account to evaluate whether or not a life is truly good. Objective evaluation is the kind to which Sarot thinks *eudaimonia* is directed. Human lives have potentials, and the excellent life is one that actualizes those potentials. But the potentials are not simply chosen, they exist as possibilities in their own right.[37]

Sarot observes that a subjectively "happy life need not be meaningful, or good, and a happy person does not necessarily flourish or experience salvation." Objective standards are required to evaluate lives as meaningful, good, flourishing, or saved, and he identifies "evaluation by objective standards," as the "proper domain for theologians."[38] The specific objective evaluation to which theology should be directed is, for Sarot, the meaning of life, which cannot be properly examined using either subjective or basic standards.[39] Sarot says these three levels of standards are frequently confused, but he argues they should be kept distinct. Certainly, basic standards of life (such as health, nourishment, shelter) need to be met, but they serve as means to the end of meaning, not as the end itself. Health, for instance, matters for quality of life, but having health does not guarantee meaning (nor does its loss lead inevitably to losing meaning). Sarot also argues that subjective standards fail as standards for meaning. Seeking meaning in one's own contentment alone may very well result in discontentment whenever desires are not met (so the approach is self-defeating). And in fact, one may gain all the contentment that one seeks and still not have a meaningful existence.[40]

Making the distinctions among levels of standards allows Sarot to explain several things. First, they explain why subjective standards alone so often seem insufficient for evaluating life—for instance why we sometimes think, "You can't *really* be happy if you live like that." They further explain why that kind of judgment is not really about happiness

37. Ibid., 5–9.
38. Ibid., 8.
39. Ibid., 16.
40. Ibid., 16–22.

as personal contentment but something else (namely, what counts as a good life). They also show why subjective and basic standards fall short of providing meaning. These distinctions are useful for analysis, but theologians would not want to say that the different levels have no significance for each other. In theology, objective standards for meaning have implications for the other two levels. To see those implications, let us examine what John Wesley's theology of happiness might have to say about each level.

WESLEY'S THEOLOGY AND THE NEW STUDY OF HAPPINESS

Wesley is not at all unique among Christian theologians in believing that Christian faith leads to helping the disadvantaged secure their basic needs. As we have seen, Wesley refers to meeting these basic standards as "happiness" (others may prefer to use the term "well-being"). Basic standards are important for happiness because satisfaction in life may be reduced if the needs for living go unmet. Christians have theological reasons for caring about meeting those needs, so theology certainly has an interest in what Sarot calls basic standards. In Christian faith, how one treats one's neighbor reflects how well one has truly grasped the meaning of God's love for the world, as well as the meaning of one's own life in relation to this God who loves the world—that is, how God expects one to use one's resources.

If basic standards are closely connected to objective standards of meaning in Christian theology, what about subjective standards? We have seen that Wesley's "religion of the heart" does deal in emotion, but the interest that Wesley's theology would have in Sarot's level of subjective standards needs to be stated carefully. With regard to what makes people feel good, Wesley might not quarrel with the idea that different things bring cheer to different people. One person may enjoy fashion, another may enjoy food, and another may enjoy prestige. Wesley acknowledges that people "seek happiness" in any number of things. He would not argue with the idea that people seek to feel happy or to be happy on their own terms. He would deny, though, that theology has nothing to say about those subjective standards. Setting our own standards for happiness is for Wesley precisely the problem because doing so shows we have not learned how to love as God loves. Wesley's theological understanding of desire is rooted in a long theological tradition, so he would not be alone in drawing a connection between objective standards of meaning and subjective standards of happiness. If being a Christian means learning to love as God loves, then even one's subjective standards for happiness will be shaped by that love. Appropriate pleasure in the world may vary—for instance one person may enjoy study more than another—but all pleasure should derive from love of God. Theology judges all subjective standards of happiness in light of God's objective standard for how the world should be enjoyed properly.

Not only Sarot, but also the psychologists discussed above focus on the subjectivity of happiness. There are several ways in which a theology of happiness resists complete subjectivity and adds objectivity. To be sure, individuals feel and those feelings depend greatly on individual perception, but Wesley (and I suspect other theologians) would want to say that what we feel is included in the transformative power of God's grace.[41] As we have seen in previous chapters, emotion is complex, and it involves cognition. Changed understanding can lead to changed emotion. How a person understands the meaning of her or his life, then, will also affect his or her emotional engagement with the world. A theology of happiness is not self-help for mood elevation. Rather, it displays the fulfillment that one may feel in living as a faithful Christian. In doing so, a theology of happiness must also describe the way a faithful Christian's life fits into God's work in the world. Wesley's theology of happiness is particularly concerned to tie happiness to love, and in his view love has to be acted out. Love of God finds expression in love of neighbor. For a Christian, one's own happiness is interrelated with the happiness of others, so it can never be merely private. Because happiness is more than just a good mood, and is so closely tied to love, it expresses itself outwardly in action. Fulfillment is experienced personally, but it is not simply subjective. Indeed, in this way of thinking, one's own happiness is intended to be a blessing to others as well as to oneself.

Nor is a theology of happiness superficial in the way that Wilson fears happiness can be. We have seen how Wesley's theology of happiness came to include a way to recognize and deal with sadness. In his view of heaviness, emotional engagement with the world is not truncated to deny hardship, but instead directs one's manner of emotional engagement with hardship toward the wholeness that God provides. The full range of one's experiences in the world belongs to Christian faith, which

41. For a thorough description of the centrality of this transformation for Wesley's theology, see Clapper, *Renewal of the Heart Is the Mission of the Church*.

helps one find meaning in any event that brings sadness. That meaning is not simply forged by individuals but is mediated by the community that hands down and celebrates the good news of God's love for us in Jesus Christ so that all our lives may be transformed. In the importance of the community, too, Christian happiness is not merely subjective.

To point out that churches have a role in mediating good news does not mean they ought to be "happiness companies," as Wilson describes them. As we have seen, both John and Charles Wesley showed a tendency to minimize negative feelings in the face of death, and this tendency does sometimes present itself among Christians. We have also seen, though, that as John Wesley continued to reflect he learned to embrace heaviness along with happiness. Churches have good reason to learn from his example because the narrative of Jesus Christ does not have just a single level of emotion. To the extent that any church denies its members the opportunity to bring all their emotions before God and understand them in that narrative, then it deserves Wilson's criticism. I once heard a religious leader say, "The psalms show us that we can pray to God in any emotion." Both Testaments that Christians regard as Scripture, then, allow us a rich emotional life rather than insisting on only feeling good. Churches need to discover, as John Wesley did, that Christian happiness does not exclude sadness. What makes the Christian narrative good news is not that negative emotions are excluded, but rather that they may be transformed by grace.

Currently, psychological study of happiness stresses subjective feeling, and it studies the feeling of individuals mostly according to their own self-report. In contrast, John Wesley's theology of happiness sets individual feeling in an objective context. As we have seen, for Wesley happiness is not just "feeling good," and the feeling that matters to him is fulfillment, which can only come from understanding what God has intended for human life and from receiving by grace the relationship with God that allows us to fulfill that intention. Even life satisfaction from using our personal strengths (Seligman's "good life") falls short of what Wesley has in mind. Rather than simply accepting what most of us think about happiness as a simple, personal feeling, theology wants to educate us about what an excellent life should be so that we may attain the appropriate happiness that goes with it.

In theology, happiness is not only fulfillment, it is also blessing. It comes to us as gift. It is not, then, a feeling under our control that we can calculatedly manipulate by following a method. Even if we may be confident that living as God would have us live leads to happiness, our confidence is in God's grace, not in our own efforts. Remembering that even our happiness begins as a gift adds to our gratitude to God.

To the extent that psychology deals with the cognitive appraisal that one's life is a good one (Peterson's definition of "life satisfaction") the field cannot ignore objective standards. Cognitive appraisal implies an understanding of what is good and an evaluation according to the values in that understanding. Indeed, Seligman's inclusion of the meaningful life as a dimension of positive psychology (as well as his personal speculation about meaning) shows that psychology is being pressed to consider more than self-reported subjective experiences. As it expands its work into matters of meaning, it undertakes more of what has traditionally been studied in philosophy and theology. It remains to be seen what positive psychology may contribute to thinking about values and virtues in a system of meaning and what kind of material commonalities or differences with theology may result.

So far, though, even psychology's own method of self-reporting shows that people who are religious tend on average to be happier than people who are not religious—probably for several reasons, such as social contact, intimate self-disclosure, having a framework of obligations that gives purpose to activity, and having a context of meaning for the events in their lives.[42] It is not by accident, then, that happiness has been a religious pursuit or that people who are religious experience happiness in a deep and lasting way. As we have seen, happiness in God has been a Christian goal and experience for centuries. The final chapter of this book will consider what it might mean for the church to take this theological pursuit seriously in its ministry.

---

42. Both Myers and Haidt cite studies that show religious involvement can contribute to happiness. Myers, *Pursuit of Happiness*, 75, and Haidt, *Happiness Hypothesis*, 88.

8

Christian Happiness and the Church

HAPPINESS HAS A LONG history as a topic in Christian theology, and a study of John Wesley's views on Christian happiness shows how robust a concept it can be. Recovery of this concept for reflection in the church can serve as a focal point to highlight the relevance and importance of Christian faith for human life. The use of language about happiness in the wider culture is becoming prevalent and familiar at the same time that the use of theological language is becoming increasingly foreign to many people, perhaps even those who call themselves Christian.[1] Because of the heritage of reflection on happiness in Christian theology, it is appropriate for the church to reclaim the language of happiness in order to communicate with people in our time. It is important, though, that this language not be simply taken over from the wider culture uncritically. As we have seen, what is being studied and promoted in popular resources is not always the kind of happiness that Christian theology has understood to be at the heart of Christian faith. While the widespread interest in happiness offers an opportunity to reengage with

---

1. For several years, I have taught a class in my local congregation for people who are joining as new members. Even those who come by transfer of membership and have been lifelong Methodists rarely know terminology (such as "prevenient grace") that is particularly associated with the Methodist tradition.

the heritage of happiness in Christianity, that heritage has to be understood and used in a way that honors the ideas of blessing and fulfillment that are at its core.

This chapter looks at some practices of ministry that would reflect a theology of happiness. They are not novel, and may even be considered generally healthy practices, but I describe them here to show how Christian happiness may be displayed, not simply in individuals, but in a congregation. This description may be of help to church leaders who want to assess, not simply the health, but also the happiness of the congregations they lead. Because of what Christian happiness is, its presence in a congregation is a sign of spiritual well-being.

TALKING ABOUT HAPPINESS

Church leaders who want to reclaim the language of happiness for congregations need to spend time explaining what Christian happiness is and what it is not. Members of congregations will have their own ideas about what happiness is and are likely to hear the language in the terms that are already familiar to them, so education in the concept matters. The resources in the tradition for talking about Christian happiness are many, and they should be used as examples of Christian reflection on a matter that is at the heart of human life. Happiness is a useful category for introducing biblical and historical study to show our connection with our past and the value of the faith that is being handed on to us ("handing on" is the very root meaning of the word *tradition*). When and why does the Bible tell us to rejoice? How could the martyrs claim to be happy as they faced death? What does happiness have to do with salvation? As people learn about these issues, they are also learning about their heritage as Christians and about the relevance of Christian faith for their lives. Studies about or sermons on happiness can be useful entry points for education about heritage that might seem dry or unimportant otherwise.

Although I do want to reclaim the language of happiness as a legitimate theological category for talking about God's work in our lives, this study of happiness shows that it is not the only legitimate theological feeling. One important reason for helping people understand Christian happiness properly is so that other feelings may also be acknowledged properly. Talking about happiness does not mean insisting that people feel good all the time. It does not mean that the "right answer" to the question "How are you?" is always "Fine," or "Great," or "Terrific."[2] It may be as important for church leaders to talk about heaviness as it is to talk about happiness. As Wesley has made clear, sorrow has its place in Christian life, and it actually truncates genuine Christian happiness to deny it. Christian happiness is gained when sorrow is transformed, not denied. So it is important to allow sorrow and other emotions to be expressed in the church.

Pastoral prayers are one way that pastors can acknowledge the wide emotional range of the people who are gathered together in a congregation. The time of lifting up concerns may be a time of lifting up genuine reactions to those concerns (sadness about a death, horror about a public shooting, helplessness in a bad economy). Sensitivity to loneliness during holidays, grief of the childless on Mother's and Father's Day, or anger in the face of injustice may also be expressed. Pastoral care is another area in which the full range of emotional life needs to be acknowledged frankly. A congregation that talks about happiness will also be able to talk about the many emotions that members feel. It brings these emotions before God, trusting in God to help bear them and to discover appropriate ways to respond to the situations that produced them.

A HAPPY CHURCH

What would a happy congregation look like? How would it promote happiness for its members? Reclaiming a theology of happiness as I have described it would not produce the "happiness companies" that Eric G. Wilson says churches have become. In fact, the churches Wilson charges with this label seem to have embraced a kind of cultural "positive thinking" rather than true Christian happiness. A recovered theology of happiness could be an important corrective for this situation. As Wesley's theology makes clear through his development of the notion of "heaviness," suppression or denial of sadness is not what Christian happiness is about. Christianity should not produce a grid that filters out all feelings or events that do not contribute to mood elevation. As Wesley makes clear, Christian happiness is not constituted by mood elevation. Instead, it is constituted by the fulfillment that comes from fitting appropriately in God's intention for human life and for all creation.

2. I have actually heard a children's sermon that claimed a Christian should always answer positively.

Christian happiness, then, means being able to account within Christian faith even for those less pleasant feelings and negative events that accompany everyday living. So a happy congregation will not be known by its exclusively smiling faces or by lack of hardship and struggle. Rather, it will be known by how well it helps members to understand the entirety of their lives within the Christian story. In a sense, the church needs to teach "scriptural happiness" in the way that early Methodists taught "scriptural holiness."

To gain scriptural happiness, one has to see the world a certain way—that is, to see it as God sees it as much as is possible for a finite human—so that one's actions in and reactions to the world are authentic expressions of Christian love. Members of a congregation have to come to understand the overarching story of the Bible, and furthermore, they have to embrace this as the story that gives coherence to the relationships and events of their lives so that they move toward a goal that is God's. In other words, they have to be able to engage the story imaginatively and thus find its relevance for their own circumstances. Through their catechesis in the narrative (that takes place in everything from worship to formal Bible study), people learn what authenticity looks like when measured against God's intention for creation. As a person learns who she or he is as a child of God, she or he also learns about the capacity to live Christianly.

On a practical level, this means that the leadership of the congregation has to teach the Christian story and demonstrate how life situations find their place in it. One important traditional help for doing so is the liturgical year that provides a framework for following the life, death, and resurrection of Jesus Christ. The liturgical year takes people through periods of introspection to examine honestly the less flattering aspects of their lives as well as to wrestle in Holy Week with the serious matters of suffering and death. Christian hope is that all these may be transformed, but they may not be transformed if they are ignored. Through the liturgical year, church tradition has provided congregations a structure for a rich and realistic account of life before God.

The liturgical year is supported by lectionary readings of the Bible, texts that have been selected because they help tell the overarching story of the Bible to the congregation. However useful these selections may be, it is also important to note that selected passages cannot tell the whole story.[3] A congregation that wants to teach that the whole of life may be embraced in Christian faith will need to find ways of exploring more of Scripture than may be possible through the lectionary alone. Whether through Bible study, congregational devotional readings, or perhaps even through special preaching series during ordinary time, members should be exposed to the fuller resources that the Bible has to offer. This exposure should include commitment to the "Old" Testament as well as the "New" Testament because both are claimed by Christians as Scripture and both provide opportunities for thinking about the many layers of human life. In fact, the stories in the oldest books of the Christian canon contain some of the most useful readings for bringing before God the messiness of life. A happy congregation will make use of the whole Bible for learning its story and for reflecting on what God would have us learn about our lives in order to find genuine happiness in God.

Successful incorporation of one's life into the Christian story involves more than just reading lots of Bible passages. The Bible is made up of many different kinds of texts that originated for different kinds of purposes. It is not, then, like a novel with a clearly delineated plot from beginning to end. It has indeed been read by the Christian community as telling an overarching story, but recognizing this story requires a particular kind of formation. A happy congregation, then, will be one that recognizes God's involvement with the world for the purpose of its redemption and renewal, and furthermore, that allows each person also to "read" the circumstances of their lives so as to recognize God's involvement in them. This formation is not a passive indoctrination into a specific substantive interpretation of any text. Rather, it should be an empowering of the people to enter into dialogue with the text so that not only may their circumstances be illumined, but their own circumstances may also illuminate or even challenge certain interpretations of the text.[4] Such dialogue will undoubtedly lead to quite different, in fact sometimes conflicting, readings among lay members, just as it does

---

3. For instance, women's stories have been underrepresented in lectionary readings. See Proctor-Smith, "Lectionaries—Principles and Problems," 84–99.

4. The freedom to interrogate not only interpretations of texts, but also the texts themselves is important, especially for passages that are frankly problematic for groups of people or for individuals in situations such as domestic abuse. Ignoring such passages neither acknowledges their consequences nor empowers readers who are affected negatively by them, but reading them does require careful mindfulness about their effects and a commitment to finding God's redemption and renewal for the affected readers.

among professionals in the clergy or academy. This situation may produce considerable discomfort, but such is the realistic consequence of engaged hermeneutics. The fact of multiple interpretations is itself an important lesson for listening carefully to what God has to say through the Bible, for taking seriously the diverse world in which we live, and for seeking to understand what God's love looks like in every situation—all of which matter for living appropriately before God. Taking the whole Bible seriously makes it particularly important for people to be able to raise critical questions and wrestle with them in the light of their faith. I have written about this kind of engagement more fully in another resource, but the important thing to note here is that the community has a responsibility to equip people for this dialogue.[5] Without such equipping, their ability to connect the Christian story with their personal stories, and thus their Christian happiness, will be diminished. A happy congregation, then, will promote biblical literacy, not simply knowing information about what the Bible contains or the ability to locate passages quickly, but also having some hermeneutical aptitude that allows them to see the relevance of these ancient texts for their present living.[6]

A commitment to such dialogue with the text means that preaching will not try to convince the congregation of any particular interpretation, but will instead open up questions that may be pondered in and through the events of daily life. To do this, the preacher will have to be honest about her or his own struggles with the text. The openness to reveal where the text connects with the preacher's own life displays a kind of vulnerability that may not always be comfortable, but if happiness is gained through fitting one's life to God's vision for the world, then hearers are helped by seeing where the attempt to fit produces tension as well as how a good fit may finally be gained from working through the tension. Of course, preaching with this kind of honesty presupposes that the preacher is serious about her or his life before God and is growing in love. In other words, the preacher must be pursuing scriptural happiness in order to lead the congregation in such a pursuit.

Preaching will also have to be attentive to what is happening in the world. If the perspective that the Christian story wants to bring people

5. See Lancaster, *Women and the Authority of Scripture*, especially chapter 5.

6. For an account of how ancient traditions have such relevance in a vital community of faith, see Clutterbuck, *Handing on Christ*. For reflection about what "biblical literacy" involves, see Swenson, "Overcoming Scriptural Illiteracy."

to see is about God's involvement in the world for its renewal and re-demption, then events throughout the world and in every corner of life from business to parenting ought to be potential sources for seeing that involvement. To preach with an awareness of what is going on in the world, though, does not mean simply preaching topical sermons. It is not enough to talk about current events or trends. Such talk must be grounded in theological insight. Preachers, then, need not only to be informed about what is taking place in the world, but they also need to cultivate their ability to see God in every event. This ability may be honed by practicing seeing God in the messy or mundane events reported in Scripture. Asking "Where is God in this?" or "What would this issue look like if God's will were done here?" are important steps in forming the perspective on the world that allows us to ask these questions about the events in our own personal lives.

If the Christian story is being presented to the congregation in an inviting and engaging way, then the members of the congregation will display an eagerness to learn more about this story. They will want to study their Bibles, they will want to talk with one another about the in-sights into their lives that such study gives them, and they will engage the preacher in conversation about the sermons. Their eagerness is a sign that they want to hear God "speak" through Scripture, and that they want to be attentive hearers.

A HAPPY CHURCH IS A HOLY CHURCH

One of the ironies about the pursuit of happiness is that seeking it direct-ly may make it more elusive. Constant attention to the questions "Am I happy?" or "Will this make me happy?" may actually have the effect of raising anxiety about attaining happiness or of getting distracted by cal-culating reward. One of the lessons of the early Methodist movement is that members were encouraged to engage in holiness activities, not hap-piness activities. John Wesley did discern in the Beatitudes a "method" for practicing the "art of happiness" but the explicit way of following this method was to live a holy life, which meant living as one was created to be, in the image of God. A holy life, then, was one of authenticity and integrity according to God's original intent for human nature. The emphasis was on living a life of authenticity before God, and happiness followed from that.

This emphasis can be seen by the mission that early Methodism embraced—to spread scriptural holiness throughout the land. Membership in a society, as we have seen, required engaging in activities that cultivated holiness and avoiding activities that countered it. The accountability of sharing in small groups fostered a self-criticism and honesty that were needed for living truthfully before God. This accountability was especially important because these practices were expected to be carried out in the midst of daily life, not in removal from "the world." What Methodists expected was authentic living in the image of God every day, under the normal stresses of life. They believed this way of living would lead to Christian happiness, and, as we have seen, they could attest that it did indeed do so.

A church can promote happiness, then, by following the lead of these early Methodist societies to gain happiness through holiness. In our time, though, the language of holiness is much more foreign and heard much less positively than the language of happiness, so it may be necessary to speak differently than the early societies did in order to do what they did. A church that wants to promote Christian happiness today may speak instead, for instance, about authentic living before God. It should acknowledge that authentic living is not easy under everyday circumstances, so it should provide help to its members for such living. That assistance has many facets, including explicit encouragement of activities that strengthen members in spiritual growth, and explicit discouragement of activities that undermine such growth. The church should also provide accountability structures in which honest self-examination can take place. Sharing in small groups is particularly effective for this accountability because people committed to the work of living authentically before God build relationships and may share examples and testimonies (of both their stumbling and their succeeding) with each other. Shared personal experiences serve as reminders and motivations for loving as God loves, especially when it is difficult to do so. Accountability may also occur in other ways (for instance, acts of confession in worship or with a priest, minister, or spiritual director).

It is important to remember, though, that for accountability structures to function well, formation of a value system must also take place. Learning to value creation as God values it is essential to having a standard by which wrongdoing or mistakes and failures may be recognized and admitted, so the shaping of desires should be a central activity of a happy church. For this reason, the designation *scriptural* happiness matters. The shaping of desires takes place in the context of learning the Christian story and finding one's place in it, as I have described above. Being holy or authentic, then, requires much more than performing designated activities. It fundamentally means reflecting the image of God through loving as God loves.

The shaping of desire clearly has a cognitive dimension for which explicit teaching matters, but because desire is felt on such a deep level in our lives, other activities that engage more dimensions of the self may be even more effective. Times of worship offer many opportunities for such engagement. Singing, for instance, can be an especially useful tool for formation because the rhythms and patterns of music resonate so deeply in our bodies. It has the capacity, then, to touch our emotions, to order our experiences, and even to help us understand more clearly.[7] The synchronicity of breathing together and staying in time with other singers makes singing a communal spiritual practice.[8] We can take songs with us as we leave, humming the tune or singing the words, so their formative effects extend beyond the worship service itself. For these reasons, church leaders need to give special attention to the values and attitudes that are being reinforced through music that is used in worship.[9] Contemplative prayer, a quiet time of listening for God and enjoying relationship with God, can also connect us with God in a deeply formational way. Church leaders, then, need to help people see prayer as something more than making requests of God. The time we spend simply in God's presence matters greatly for how we come to share God's vision for the world. Partaking of Holy Communion is another way of sharing in God's presence and vision. As Eucharist, it is explicitly a time of gratitude (one of Wesley's ways of designating true religion), and because the acts of eating and drinking together involve our bodies so directly, we may be "fed" on multiple levels. A happy church will be at-

---

7. For a description of how music works in us, and even helps us gain our identities, see Saliers, *A Song to Sing, a Life to Live.*

8. Wallace, "Singing as Communal Spiritual Practice." This brief article gives tips for making congregational singing more effective.

9. We have seen how important Charles Wesley's hymns were for teaching about happiness and holiness in the early Methodist movement, and even when more modern songs are used the goal should be to use music that is capable of conveying God's vision for the world upon which our own vision should be modeled.

tentive to the role that worship plays in the way we learn to relate to God and thus also to God's world.

Leaders who want a happy church will look for ways of helping members of the congregation express to God what is going on in their lives. Worship may become an important place where this expression can happen. Such expression may take the form of verbal articulation in prayers, song, and preaching, but it may also occur in rituals that allow members of the congregation to enact what is on their minds, for instance through lighting candles, taking something to the altar, and so on. Creating an atmosphere for such expression requires both empathy and imagination. Worship planners must be able to put themselves in the position of the people in the congregation in order to imagine what may need to be expressed, and they must also be able to create opportunities that will draw people in to participate. By allowing expression of thoughts and feelings, worship places these deep areas of our lives before God. Participants then have a chance to imagine seeing those elements of themselves as God sees them. As this perspective is gained, they then can learn to want what God wants for them. Carefully planned rituals, then, do not simply allow personal expression but also shape aspirations.

Worship that has brought us into the presence of God and helped us share God's vision for the world should lead us out into God's world to show God's love there.[10] If worship helps us focus on gratitude and love of God, active service allows us to demonstrate love of neighbor (or benevolence, the other essential designation of Wesley's true religion). A church that is successfully helping its members live authentically before God will provide many opportunities for its members to show their love in concrete ways by addressing the needs of their local community and of the world. If members of a congregation are experiencing a vital relationship with God in such a way that they know the joyful fulfillment of

---

10. At the time of the writing of this book, there is a trend in the United States of congregations using the Sunday morning worship time for doing service in the community. If this trend indicates that worship is seen as dispensable, then it is unfortunate. I am certainly in favor of demonstrating the vital link between worship and service, and such a link could appropriately be made in a Sunday activity (preferably after worship, not in place of it). It is important, though, not to make a service activity appear to be a substitute for worship. Substituting a service activity for worship undercuts the message that making ourselves available to be in God's presence is just as important as what we do. We do not work ourselves into relationship with God. Furthermore, without worship, our service may become a duty instead of a joy.

being blessed by God's grace, then they will want to be a blessing to others. They will avail themselves of these opportunities often and gladly. Because they may be even more aware of the needs of the community than the church leaders are, members may be the driving force for naming and cultivating opportunities for service. A happy church shares its happiness with others in every way that it can.

Sharing happiness includes sharing the source of that happiness, namely, the trusting faith that is at the heart of one's relationship with God. Members who are happy in God will want to tell others why they are happy in God. Because they know the Christian story, they can share that story, along with testimony of how the grace of God has filled their lives with love. If they have been taught that happiness does not deny heaviness, they will be attentive to the real struggles that people face every day. They can share the difference that God has made for their own struggles, and they can offer Christ as genuine transformation, not denial of reality. A happy church will be an invitational church, seeking to share the love of God with all those who are open to receive.

A happy church will not only be invitational, it will also be hospitable to all those who answer the invitation. It will be welcoming of those who seek God regardless of how different they may be. Because true Christian happiness can accept heaviness, a happy church can accept those who suffer heaviness—whether that be short or long term, caused by unemployment, illness, disability, mental illness, or any of the other major hurdles in life. A church that is happy because of the love of God will show the love of God. If its message about happiness is that we are embraced and not abandoned by God even in times of heaviness, then it will demonstrate that message by not abandoning those who find themselves in situations that cause heaviness. Instead, the church welcomes them, makes its resources accessible to them, and finds opportunities for their participation in the life of the congregation.

As the Christian narrative becomes more truly their own, Christians gain an inner authenticity in their lives before God. The cognitive aspect of their emotions will be affected as they learn what to be happy, or angry, or compassionate, or concerned *about*. When this Christianly shaped inner life serves to motivate outward actions in service to others, those acts also gain authenticity by being rooted in a genuine Christian self-understanding with desires that have been conformed to God. The capacity to live Christianly both can and should be realized, and when it is, happiness results.[11] It should be noted that the realization of this capacity depends not merely on the church's catechesis or on an individual's imaginative engagement, but primarily on God's grace. It is God's grace that allows one to know oneself as a child of God, that enables the church's teaching to be effective in the lives of its members, and that activates one's imagination to connect Scripture to one's life. God's gift of empowerment is blessing that enables our participation so that we may be fulfilled.

If this kind of happiness is truly coming to expression in a congregation, members will be eager to engage in those activities that encourage or display authentic life before God. They will want to study the Bible, they will seek out opportunities to worship God, they will look for ways to express to others the love of God that they themselves have come to know. The more they know the blessing of grace in their own lives, the more they will want their lives to be a blessing to others. They will be eager to express their gratitude to God and to share with others their stories of their relationship with God, and they will be eager to share their resources with those in need in order to make God's love visible.

A theology of happiness helps make clear the blessing and fulfillment that Christian faith has to offer. The pursuit of this happiness is an ancient concern, and the general interest in happiness makes it timely to reclaim the concern as our own. If offering Christ to the world means offering people a chance to be happy in God, then the church has something to say that people may truly want to hear.

---

11. As Wesley said, interpreting Phil 2:12–13, "For, first God works; therefore you *can* work. Secondly, God works; therefore you *must* work." John Wesley, *Works*, 3:199–209.

Bibliography

Allen, William. *A Glass of Justification, or the Work of Faith with Power*. London: Printed by G. Dawson, for F. Smith, 1658.

The American Heritage Dictionary of the English Language. Boston: Houghton Mifflin, 1992.

Aquinas, Thomas. *Summa Theologica*. Translated by the Fathers of the English Dominican Province. New York: Benzinger Brothers, 1947.

Augustine. *The City of God against the Pagans IV*. Loeb Classical Library. Cambridge: Harvard University Press, 1966.

———. *Confessions*. In *Augustine: Confessions and Enchiridion*. Translated by Albert C. Outler. Library of Christian Classics 7. Philadelphia: Westminster, 1955.

———. *On the Trinity, Books 8–15*. Translated by Gareth B. Matthews. Cambridge Texts in the History of Philosophy. Cambridge: Cambridge University Press, 2006.

Babcock, William S. "Cupiditas and Caritas: The Early Augustine on Love and Fulfillment." In *Augustine Today*, edited by Richard John Neuhaus, 1–34. Encounter Series. Grand Rapids: Eerdmans, 1993.

Balguy, John. *Silvius' Examination of Certain Doctrines Lately Taught, and Defended by the Reverend Mr. Stebbing*. London: Printed for J. Roberts, 1718.

Baxter, Richard Baxter. *How Far Holinesse Is the Design of Christianity*. London: Printed for Nevill Simons, 1671.

Bilger, Audrey. *Laughing Feminism: Subversive Comedy in Frances Burney, Maria Edgeworth, and Jane Austen*. Detroit: Wayne State University Press, 1998.

Birkbeck, George. "Introduction." In *History of Rasselas: Prince of Abyssinia*, by Samuel Johnson, 9–33. Oxford: Clarendon, 1967.

Bragge, Francis. *Of Undissembled and Persevering Religion: In Several Sermons upon the Following Subjects*. London: Printed by W. D. for John Wyat, 1713.

Brown, Ruth Allison. *S. Aureli Augustini De Beata Vita: A Translation with an Introduction and Commentary*. Washington, DC: Catholic University of America, 1944.

Brümmer, Vincent. "Preface." In *Happiness, Well-Being and the Meaning of Life; A Dialogue of Social Science and Religion*, edited by Vincent Brümmer and Marcel Sarot. Kampen, The Netherlands: Kok Pharos, 1996.

Bunyan, John. *A Defence of the Doctrine of Justification by Faith in Jesus Christ.* 1672. Oxford: Oxford University Press, 1989. Also in vol. 2 of *The Works of John Bunyan,* vol. 2: *Experimental, Doctrinal, and Practical,* ed. George Offor. Edinburgh: Banner of Truth, 1991.

Charry, Ellen. *God and the Art of Happiness.* Grand Rapids: Eerdmans, 2010.

Chilcote, Paul Wesley, ed. *Her Own Story: Autobiographical Portraits of Early Methodist Women.* Nashville: Kingswood Books, 2001.

Clapper, Gregory S. *John Wesley on Religious Affections: His Views on Experience and Emotion and Their Role in the Christian Life and Theology.* Metuchen, NJ, and London: Scarecrow Press, 1989.

———. "John Wesley's Language of the Heart." *Wesleyan Theological Journal* 44, no. 2 (Fall 2009) 94–102.

———. *The Renewal of the Heart Is the Mission of the Church.* Eugene, OR: Cascade Books, 2009.

Clement of Alexandria. *The Rich Man's Salvation.* In *The Exhortation to the Greeks, The Rich Man's Salvation, and the Fragment of an Address Entitled to the Newly Baptized.* Translated by G. W. Butterworth. Loeb Classical Library, reprint 1960.

———. *Stromata.* In *Clemens Alexandrinus,* vol. 2, edited by Otto Stählin. Berlin: Akademie-Verlag, 1960.

Clement of Rome. *Second Letter of Clement to the Corinthians.* In *The Apostolic Fathers I.* Loeb Classical Library. Cambridge: Harvard University Press, 2003.

Clutterbuck, Richard. *Handing on Christ: Rediscovering the Gift of Christian Doctrine.* London: Epworth, 2009.

Collins, Ken. *John Wesley: A Theological Journey.* Nashville: Abingdon, 2003.

———. *A Real Christian: The Life of John Wesley.* Nashville: Abingdon, 1999.

Culverwel, Nathaneal. *The White Stone or a Learned and Choice Treatise of Assurance: Very Useful for All, but Especially Weak Believers.* In *An Elegant, and Learned Discourse of the Light of Nature: With several other Treatises.* London: Printed by Roycroft, for William Grantham, 1661.

Davies, Rupert E. "Introduction." In *The Methodist Societies: History, Nature, and Design,* vol. 9, edited by Rupert E. Davies. In *The Bicentennial Edition of the Works of John Wesley,* 9:1–29. Editor-in-chief Frank Baker. Nashville: Abingdon, 1989.

DeHeer, Cornelius. *Makar—Eudaimon—Olbios—Eutyches: A Study of the Semantic Field Denoting Happiness in Ancient Greek to the End of the 5th Century B.C.* Amsterdam: Adolf M. Hakkert, 1969.

Dixon, Thomas. *From Passions to Emotions: The Creation of a Secular Psychological Category.* Cambridge: Cambridge University Press, 2003.

Doddridge, P. *The Rise and Progress of Religion in the Soul: Illustrated in a Course of Serious and Practical Addresses, suited to Persons of every Character and Circumstance: With a Devout Meditation or Prayer added to each Chapter.* London: Printed for J. Waugh and J. Bucelard, 1748.

Edwards, Jonathan. *A Treatise Concerning Religious Affections.* In *The Work of Jonathan Edwards,* vol. 2, edited by John E. Smith. New Haven: Yale University Press, 1959.

Flanders, Judith. *Consuming Passions: Leisure and Pleasure in Victorian Britain.* London: Harper Press, 2006.

Flavel, John. *The Touchstone of Sincerity or the Signs of Grace, and Symptomes of Hypocrisie, Opened in a Practical Treatise upon Rev. 3.17,18.* London: Printed by M. White, for F. Tynton, 1679.

Fowler, Edward. *The Design of Christianity*. London: Printed by F. Tyler and R. Holt, for R. Royston, 1671.

Gatrell, Vic. *City of Laughter: Sex and Satire in Eighteenth-Century London*. New York: Walker & Company, 2006.

Gay, John. "Concerning the Fundamental Principle of Virtue or Morality." In *The English Philosophers from Bacon to Mill*, edited by Edwin A. Burtt. The Modern Library. New York: Random House, 1967.

Gilbert, Daniel. *Stumbling on Happiness*. New York: Alfred A. Knopf, 2006.

Haidt, Jonathan, *The Happiness Hypothesis: Finding Modern Truth in Ancient Wisdom*. New York: Basic Books, 2006.

Herodotus. *The History*. Loeb Classical Library. Cambridge: Harvard University Press, 1960.

Hurst, John Fletcher. *John Wesley the Methodist: A Plain Account of His Life and Work by a Methodist Preacher*. New York: Eaton & Mains, 1903.

Jackson, Thomas, ed. *The Lives of Early Methodist Preachers, Chiefly Written by Themselves*. London: John Mason, various dates.

Johnson, Samuel. *A Dictionary of the English Language in which the Words are Deduced from their Originals, and Illustrated in their Different Significations by Examples from the Best Writers, to which are prefixed a History of the Language and an English Grammar*. London: Printed by W. Strahan, 1755. Reprint New York, AMS Press, 1967.

————. *History of Rasselas: Prince of Abyssinia*. Oxford: Clarendon, 1967.

Knox, Alexander. "Remarks on the Life and Character of John Wesley," in *The Life of Wesley and the Rise and Progress of Methodism with notes by the Late Samuel Taylor Coleridge Esq., and Remarks on the Life and Character of John Wesley by the late Alexander Knox, Esq.*, by Robert Southey, ed. Charles Cuthbert Southey. London: Printed for Longman, Hurst, Rees, Orme, and Brown, 1820.

Lancaster, Sarah Heaner. *Women and the Authority of Scripture: A Narrative Approach*. Harrisburg, PA: Trinity Press International, 2002.

Lee, Umphrey. *The Historical Backgrounds of Early Methodist Enthusiasm*. New York: Columbia University Press, 1931.

Locke, John. *An Essay Concerning Human Understanding*. Edited by Alexander Campbell Fraser. New York: Dover Publications, 1959.

Lyles, Albert M. *Methodism Mocked: The Satiric Reaction to Methodism in the Eighteenth Century*. London: Epworth, 1960.

Maddox, Randy L. *Responsible Grace: John Wesley's Practical Theology*. Nashville: Kingswood Books, 1994.

————. "A Change of Affections: The Development, Dynamics, and Dethronement of John Wesley's Heart Religion." In *'Heart Religion' in the Methodist Tradition and Related Movements*, edited by Richard B. Steele, 3–31. Lanham, MD, and London: Scarecrow Press, 2001.

Marcion. *The Martyrdom of Polycarp*. In *The Apostolic Fathers I*. Loeb Classical Library. Cambridge: Harvard University Press, 2003.

McMahon, Darrin M. *Happiness: A History*. New York: Atlantic Monthly Press, 2006.

Miles, Rebekah. "The Instrumental Role of Reason." In *Wesley and the Quadrilateral: Renewing the Conversation*, edited by W. Stephen Gunter et al. Nashville: Abingdon, 1997.

Murlin, John. "The Life of John Murlin." In *The Lives of Early Methodist Preachers, Chiefly Written by Themselves*, vol. 2, edited by Thomas Jackson. London: John Mason, 1837.

Myers, David G. *The Pursuit of Happiness: Who Is Happy—and Why?* New York: William Morrow, 1992.

Nussbaum, Martha. *The Fragility of Goodness: Luck and Ethics in Greek Tragedy and Philosophy*. Cambridge: Cambridge University Press, 1986.

Outler, Albert C. *Evangelism and Theology in the Wesleyan Spirit*. Nashville: Discipleship Resources, 1996.

———. "Introduction." In *Sermons*, in *The Bicentennial Works of John Wesley*, 1:1–100. Editor-in-chief Frank Baker. Nashville: Abingdon, 1984.

Parry, Richard. "Ancient Ethical Theory." In The Stanford Encyclopedia of Philosophy, 2004 edition, edited by Edward N. Zalta. Online: http://plato.stanford.edu/entries/ethics-ancient/.

Peterson, Christopher. *A Primer in Positive Psychology*. New York: Oxford University Press, 2006.

Plato. *Euthyphro, Apology, Crito, Phaedo, Phaedrus*. Translated by Harold North Fowler. Loeb Classical Library. Cambridge: Harvard University Press, 1971 reprint.

Proctor-Smith, Marjorie. "Lectionaries—Principles and Problems: Alternative Perspectives/" *Studia Liturgica* 22, no. 1 (1992) 84–99.

Reddy, William M. *The Navigation of Feeling: A Framework for the History of Emotion*. Cambridge: Cambridge University Press, 2001.

Rubin, Gretchen. *The Happiness Project: Or, Why I Spent a Year Trying to Sing in the Morning, Clean My Closets, Fight Right, Read Aristotle, and Generally Have More Fun*. New York: Harper Collins, 2009.

Runyon, Theodore. *The New Creation: John Wesley's Theology Today*. Nashville: Abingdon, 1998.

Saliers, Don, and Emily Saliers. *A Song to Sing, a Life to Live: Reflections on Music as Spiritual Practice*. The Practice of Faith Series, edited by Dorothy C. Bass. San Francisco: Jossey-Bass, 2005.

Sarot, Marcel. "Introduction." In *Happiness, Well-Being and the Meaning of Life: A Dialogue of Social Science and Religion*, edited by Vincent Brümmer and Marcel Sarot. Kampen, The Netherlands: Kok Pharos, 1996.

Seligman, Martin E. P. *Authentic Happiness: Using the New Positive Psychology to Realize Your Potential for Lasting Fulfillment*. New York: Free Press, 2002.

Seligman, Martin E. P., et al. "Positive Psychology Progress: Empirical Validation of Interventions." *American Psychologist* 60, no. 5 (2005) 410–21.

Swenson, Kristin. "Overcoming Scriptural Illiteracy." *The Christian Century*, November 3, 2009, 22–25.

Telford, John. *The Life of John Wesley*. London: Wesleyan Methodist Book Room, 1902.

Trapp, Michael. *Philosophy in the Roman Empire: Ethics, Politics, and Society*. Burlington, VT: Ashgate, 2007.

Wagner, Rich. *The Myth of Happiness: Discovering a Joy You Never Thought Possible*. Grand Rapids: Zondervan, 2007.

Wallace, Robin Knowles. "Singing as Communal Spiritual Practice." Cokesbury's Worship Connection. Cokesbury Bookstore (copyright 2010, United Methodist Publishing House). Online: http://worshipconnection.cokesbury.com/content.aspx?dyn=1751.

Walton, Brad. *Jonathan Edwards, Religious Affections and the Puritan Analysis of True Piety, Spiritual Sensation and Heart Religion.* Studies in American Religion 7. Lewiston, NY: Edward Mellen, 2002.

Watson, David Lowes. *The Early Methodist Class Meeting: Its Origin and Significance.* Nashville: Discipleship Resources, 1985. Reprint, Eugene, OR, Wipf and Stock, 2002.

Wesley, Charles. "And Is the Struggle Past?" In *Funeral Hymns,* edited by Charles Wesley, #10, 14–15. London: Strahan, 1746.

———. Charles Wesley's Published Verse. Duke Center for Studies in the Wesleyan Tradition. Online: http://www.divinity.duke.edu/initiatives-centers/cswt/wesley-texts/charles-wesley (All hymns cited are available here.)

———. "Happy the Man who Jesus knows." In *Hymns for Children,* edited by Charles Wesley, #5, 7. Bristol: Farley, 1763.

———. "Happy the Souls to Jesus join'd." In *Hymns on the Lord's Supper,* edited by Charles Wesley, #96, 83–84. Bristol: Farley, 1745.

———. "Maker, Saviour of Mankind." In *Hymns for Children,* edited by Charles Wesley, #15, 15–16. Bristol: Farley, 1763.

———. "Rejoice for a brother deceas'd." In *Funeral Hymns,* edited by Charles Wesley #2, 3. London: Strahan, 1746.

———. "Thou Hidden Source of Calm Repose." In *Hymns and Sacred Poems,* edited by Charles Wesley, #31, 1:245–46. Bristol: Farley, 1749.

———. "Who believes the tidings?" In *Hymns and Sacred Poems,* edited by Charles Wesley, #8, 1:36–37. Bristol: Farley, 1749

Wesley, John. *The Bicentennial Edition of the Works of John Wesley* [35 volumes projected]. Editor-in-chief Frank Baker. Nashville: Abingdon, 1984ff.

———. *Explanatory Notes upon the New Testament.* 1976 ed. Reprint, London: Epworth, 2000.

———. *A Plain Account of Christian Perfection As Believed and Taught by the Reverend Mr. John Wesley from the year 1725 to the year 1777.* Kansas City, MO: Beacon Hill Press of Kansas City, 1966.

———. *Sermons.* Edited by Albert C. Outler. Vols. 1–4 of *The Bicentennial Edition of the Works of John Wesley.* Editor-in-chief Frank Baker. Nashville: Abingdon, 1984–1987.

Wills, Garry. *Inventing America: Jefferson's Declaration of Independence.* Garden City, NY: Doubleday, 1978.

Wilson, Eric G. *Against Happiness: In Praise of Melancholy.* New York: Farrar, Straus, and Giroux, 2008.

———. "In Praise of Melancholy." *The Chronicle of Higher Education,* January 18, 2008, B11–B14.